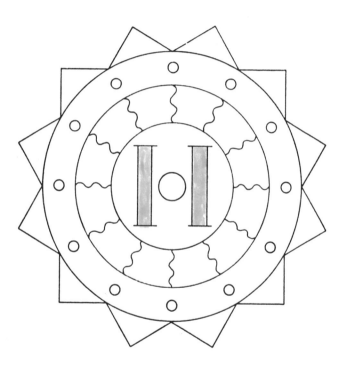

THE STILL
SMALL VOICE

Robert Wall Crary

Rishis Institute of Metaphysics, Inc.
21933 Euclid Avenue,
Cleveland, Ohio 44117-1552

ISBN 0-914711-06-7
Library of Congress Catalog Card Number: 92-82655

A publication of
Rishis Institute of Metaphysics
21933 Euclid Avenue Euclid, Ohio 44117-1552

Printed in the United States of America

I gratefully dedicate this work to Raymond A. Cassidy, our beloved teacher and founder of Rishis Institute of Metaphysics, whose life and teachings inspired the essence of all that is contained herein.

I further dedicate it to the service of the great Masters of Light, the Brothers of the great White Lodge, and all the Forces of Light, who are working unceasingly to help lift the humanity of this planet into the deeper and higher spiritual awareness—the full consciousness of the Higher Self within the soul of every human being—all to the glory of God, our Divine Creator.

Finally, I dedicate it to the many thousands of students who have studied at Rishis Institute of Metaphysics and to the millons of souls on this earth who seek the Higher Life. We send them our Love, and we rejoice in the knowledge that the Light of the Christ Self in each of them shines forth in an ever greater measure of divine guidance and protection.

ACKNOWLEDGMENTS

I extend my sincere gratitude to Sandy Gentile for her patience and diligence in typing the proof and final copies of the manuscript for this book. She has done beautiful work.

The drawings are creations of JoAnne Koenig. I want to express my genuine appreciation to her for providing these fitting works of art. In their original simplicity, they convey to the viewer a recurring message that pervades each chapter—the priceless value of the Silence and Meditation to travelers of the Path of Light as they journey along their Way in spiritual unfoldment to their Destiny of Spiritual Mastery.

The author of the poems in this volume is Frances Ellen Crary. I extend to her this due recognition and my gratitude for her permission to include them herein. As usual, her poems are simply yet exquisitely finished in her unique style, and they make a valuable and novel addition to this work.

THE VOICE WITHIN MY SOUL

Softly, clear as a bird cry on a bright morning,
And as easily ignored,
The Voice within my soul speaks out of Silence,
Like music breaking loose, longing.

Why is there fear? Why doubt?
My Heart strives to hear, to respond,
But I silence Her with disbelief.
I turn avoiding. What is the danger?

If I listen to Her—to Heart,
All the sacred patterns of history,
All the rules that have held safety for us,
Will be broken, will be in question.
How shall I bear to see myself?

All that I have learned in slow questing,
Seems as if a darkness, a foolishness,
Before this new Light,
Light that speaks from Silence! Light that
Illumines even as it fades away old limits.
And I resist because of my unwilling vision.

But Heart yearns to listen, respond!
Mind is divided, caught in conflict.
One part reaches up, with the joy of new Vision,
The other shrinks down, holds itself blind.
For to hear-see means to know my own depths,
As well as to know of human holiness and evil.
I do not know how to bear either.

Unable to hide, I must hasten to ask,
"Oh God within who speaks, help me to bear
All that I hear. Help me to *know*
Of Wonder, of Love, and of Wisdom
Without fear, with joy and acceptance!

"Oh Spirit of Love, help me to bear the Light,
The knowledge that I may free my Heart
And let it soar beyond me, drawing me behind,
Into Vision. Let my Heart inform me,
My Inner Voice, waken me, lead me to
  Realization!"

FRANCES ELLEN CRARY

CONTENTS

FOREWORD

As you read what is written herein, listen to the very depth of your soul and interpret these words as the Voice of your God Self within the Temple of your own Being—the Voice of the real You, the Spiritual Counterpart of your own Individuality, your Master Supreme to know and follow. In so doing, you will not consider this voice a human one. Instead, you will let any awareness of mortal utterance fade into the background of your mind and, in its place, permit the Presence of God within you to stand forth vividly in your consciousness and reveal to you the following spiritual message it bears for you who are ready and able to recognize and accept its reality in your heart and mind. The more you read it in this manner, the more you will build the substance of this message deeper into your consciousness; and you will also develop a greater ability to detect, correctly interpret, and heed the guidance that the Still, Small Voice of this Presence is ceaselessly giving to you every day.

RISHIS INSTITUTE OF METAPHYSICS

CREDO

IT IS MY DESIRE TO SIT CALMLY UPON
THE THRONE IN THE TEMPLE OF
MY OWN BODY BETWEEN THE
TWO GREAT PILLARS OF
POSITIVE AND NEGATIVE VIBRATION,
BALANCING THEM TO THE POINT
WHERE I CAN RADIATE THROUGH
MY TEMPLE OF LIGHT,
TO ALL WHOM I CONTACT,
THE WONDERFUL PEACE, POISE,
POWER, WISDOM, LOVE,
AND HARMONY OF GOD.

CHAPTER I

The Still Small Voice

To you who hearken to My Voice, I bring a message of Light—a message of My Light, My Truth, My Peace. I speak only in Love. Your heart and mind are drawn to Me now for reasons that are individually your own. You may yearn for a deeper meaning in life. You may be feeling any one of the many pains that life can bring. Problems or questions may demand solutions or answers that you cannot find. Spiritual or material needs may be unfilled. Whatever the reasons may be, they are blessings in disguise. They are teaching you to turn to Me so I can lead you into a higher spiritual consciousness.

Who Am I? I Am the Still, Small Voice of God within you. Even as I Am with you now, I have been with you throughout the ages of your past; and I will be with you always into eternity. I Am speaking to you from the Inner Recesses of your Being.

I have come to you many times as an impression—sometimes so strong that you interpreted it as spoken words—guiding, inspiring, teaching, and leading you onward and upward to Me and to My Light. Do you recognize, then, that I Am your Higher Spiritual Self within you? If you do, listen to what I have to tell you and follow implicitly what I say.

I have come to you to reveal the Way of Life that will bring you happiness and success in everything you do. I want to give you the answers to all your questions and the solutions to all your problems.

You say, how can anyone answer all questions or solve all problems? Does it seem unrealistic to you? If you are thinking of the human mind and the human consciousness alone, then, truly, it is not practical. But if you recognize My Presence within you and, therefore, in your life, then it is most realistic. In fact, it is the most pragmatic thing in Life, and so in your life, to the degree that you positively respond to Me and to My Light, in the proportion that you recognize My Presence within you and follow in the Path of My Light as I, your Inner Guidance, direct you. Yes, I Am the Still, Small Voice that you have heard so much about, but to which you have paid little conscious attention in the past. Then, you were not ready; but now, to the extent that you recognize the reality of My Presence, you are ready. And to the degree that you follow My

Guidance will I come into your awareness in ever-greater measure until, finally, you learn to follow Me completely—and only Me—in all of your thinking, speaking, acting, and feeling. Then, I will abide supreme in your life and will gradually enable you to rise above all conditions of the world, yes, answering all your questions and solving all your problems. I will lead you to become Master of your "self" and of all conditions in the material world.

Yet, it is very important that you realize this will not be easy. However, it will be just as easy as *you* make it. It will take everything you have to accomplish it, *and sometimes more.* It will require a strong self-discipline and a great, steadfast desire to change yourself to become more than you are or have ever been. You will need perseverance, determination, and utmost patience with yourself and others. The cultivation of the virtues, such as love, kindness, goodness, honesty, forgiveness, compassion, happiness, joy, and all the others, will be required. It takes a strong, courageous soul to travel the Path of Light.

It is true that you cannot do it alone. You can do it, however, in response to Me and to My Light—and in and through Me is the only Way—because I Am the Christ, the Spirit of God, within you. I Am Perfection, and to the extent that you respond to My Light do you come into the awareness of My Consciousness, into the perfection of My Being. By degrees, you learn to rise above the lack and limitations of the material world in which you live and the limited awareness of your conscious mind. Now, turn your attention to Me, the Spiritual Essence of your Being within, and follow My Thought as I lead you into an awareness of My Presence, your own God Self, your Superconsciousness, within your own Temple.

As you read what is being said here, are you listening to a deep, deep presence of Being within the very depth of your own soul? Can you sense a very, very quiet, utterly still, impression—feeling—thought— coming to your conscious mind from this depth of your soul, from this sacred Inner Awareness of your consciousness? Listen, listen, listen. Can you recognize that this is the Voice of the Spiritual Essence of your Being? Are you not thrilled at the very thought of it? Can you realize that it is I, your own God Self, speaking to you? No, I Am not of the physical plane. Yet, I Am far more real than your mortal, physical body and conscious mind. I Am Eternal, Infinite, Immortal. I Am God—your individualized Spiritual Self—within the center of every cell of your body. Have you not been told that you are the Temple of God and that the Spirit of God dwells within you? So, perhaps you cannot see Me, but you *can* become aware of My Presence. You *can* hear My Still, Small Voice. I come to you as a feeling, a thought, an impression, an awareness, a realization from deep within you, utterly still and quiet—soundless—a Spiritual Voice.

To hear My Voice, your mind and emotions must attain a sufficient degree of peace and tranquility or they will be too turbulent, too loud, too coarse to sense the finer vibrations of My Voice that are constantly beckoning to you to follow Me. Of course, you understand that I Am using these printed words to reach you now so you can read with your eyes as you sense in your heart this message I Am bringing to you; but you can learn to hear My Still, Small Voice at all times speaking directly to you through your mind so that I can constantly guide your life if you will learn to become quiet and attentive enough to hear Me. In learning to do this, it is important to realize that it is your mind alone that hears My Voice and perceives My Presence.

I can speak to you through any channel that is open to Me on any plane, including the physical plane. And I can reveal My Message to you through your eyes and ears. Still, your awareness of My Truth always requires your mental and emotional response to Me *within your own Temple* before you can realize its trueness. Therefore, everything that comes to you in Truth must come through Me to your mind because I Am the Way—and the only Way. Anyone who attempts to enter My Greater

Light in any other way is a thief and a robber, an instrument of the negative force. I Am the only Way through which anyone can enter the Kingdom of Heaven. *No one* can enter therein except through Me.

Do you want the higher life, My Spiritual Life? Do you want to rise above the lack and limitations of mortality and build strong any weaknesses of your mortal being? Are you ready to learn to accept Me fully into your life and to place My Will always before your own personal will? Are you prepared to release yourself from all the negative things in this world in order to live in the positive response to My Guidance, My Light, My Love, and My Truth? You know—I have told you—I Am the Truth, the Light, the Life, and the Way. My Message is one of Divine Love.

CHAPTER II

Your Destiny

You may ask, "How can I know that the message you are bringing me is true?" The only way you can *know* the reality of My Presence and of your spiritual heritage that it is your destiny to make your Ascension into Spiritual Mastery, even as Christ, Buddha, and many others have done, is by an awareness in your heart and mind of its reality. It is your own soul's response to the Divine Mind of God that brings this knowing. When you follow its promptings, which is, in reality, your realization of Me within you, you come into a deeper and deeper perception of it as you grow in spiritual sensitivity. By degrees, you come to the place in consciousness where you simply know because you know. You know in the same way that you know when you feel love. It is an inner experience of your mind and soul. It becomes a total awareness in consciousness—the only way that your mind *can* know absolutely. It is a means of knowing that far transcends any form of knowledge that comes to you through your physical senses. Finally, in time, you become the living expression of its reality.

Still, looking more carefully, you can further understand that the Light of that knowing can seem to recede almost into obscurity in the radiant brilliance of the greater Light of a deeper awareness of My Truth. The following examples are only three of many that could be listed to show you the veracity of this statement. 1) The fact that the world is round has in present-day thinking considerably concealed the fact that it is also flat in the everyday experience of walking on its surface. The vividness of the lesser experience has in the past been so strong in the minds of the people of this civilization that it was tenaciously accepted for centuries, causing mankind to vehemently resist the greater truth that it is a sphere. 2) Many people have experienced love but to find later a greater love that caused them to feel the lesser love vastly diminished in the presence of the greater one. 3) A mind that grasps an abstract concept of God usually ceases to see a tree or the wind as his Deity. In a yet higher consciousness, however, he realizes them to be all part of the same Essence. It follows, then, that you can always achieve a deeper awareness of My Being and, thus, of your Oneness with Me.

Now, can you glimpse the fact that you and I are One? Yes, you are not aware of that in consciousness, but you can become so. I repeat to you that it is your inherent destiny to unite with Me in consciousness so that I can fulfill My Purpose through you in the harmony of this Oneness between us: you and I and God *are* ONE. Furthermore, can you realize that I Am the *real* you? You, the conscious mind and physical body, the personality, are but My Creation in the physical plane—an instrument for My Use and My Perfection. To you, My Beloved Creation, I have given free will. So, you must come to Me of your own free will, surrendering your own will to Mine, if you truly desire the freedom of Spirit and the unlimited heights in consciousness that are yours merely for the asking. Yet, the asking is much, much more than a simple spoken word. It includes the complete surrender of yourself to Me—your will to My Will, the purificiation of your soul in positive response to My Light, My Love, and My Truth, and the training and discipline of yourself to live at all times within the perfect expression of My Law. So, when you unite in consciousness with Me, My Light transforms you into a perfect Being, a Master of Light. In this union, you rise above the human into the Divine. You make your Ascension into My Light. This is your Heritage; it is your Destiny.

I have told you that I Am God, that I Am still, and that to know Me, you must be still in mind, emotions, and body. Since I Am within you, to find Me, it is necessary for you to look within yourself in stillness and listen by means of the Silence and Meditation. Then and only then can you unfalteringly hear My Still, Small Voice that is ceaselessly trying to reach and to keep your conscious attention so that I may lead you to your Destiny of Spiritual Mastery.

CHAPTER III

You and I

Know that I Am your Inner God Self. I Am the Spiritual Counterpart of your physical mind and body. It is I who created you and brought you to your present state of spiritual awareness. I have done this in order to create for My Use an instrument for My Greater Expression and for My Higher Purpose. You dwell in the material plane; I, in the Spiritual. Yet, always remember that I Am you and you are Me, although you have not yet come to My Awareness in consciousness.

You would not exist if it were not for Me; neither could I bring to Myself the expression that I desire except through you. You are an extension of My Consciousness into the material plane. You serve as an instrument, a vehicle, through which I, your Impersonal Spiritual Self, can express in the physical world in personal expression. Thus, you and I *are* really One, except that I have not yet developed your

11

sensibility to the place where you can come into conscious awareness of My Consciousness. So, to the degree that you have not yet come up to My Spiritual Consciousness, you see yourself as separate from Me. Too often, you do not even recognize My Presence because your mind and your attention are held so strongly by the experiences of the material side of life, by your indulgence in their response to your physical senses and appetites, and by the turbulence of your emotions thus engendered. Losing your attention in the appearance world and accepting it as the true reality brings about negative emotions in you, such as fear, doubt, and anxiety, that prevent you from feeling My Presence and hearing My Voice.

From the very inception of your being, I have led you into higher and higher states of consciousness. In time, I have developed in you a mind that permits you to become conscious of yourself. With this development have come many mental attributes, such as reason, willpower, understanding, memory, cognition, and many others. You began to want to know who you were, whence you came, and what your destiny was. You need but to look at the past development of mankind to see the many forms and varied expressions that this desire to know has taken. There is an almost unlimited array of religious philosophies, beliefs, and practices, each reflecting the degree of the spiritual awareness of Me in its leaders and followers. Can you recognize that all of this is My Desire in mankind that has led him to seek to come to a fuller awareness of himself and of life until he finally finds that he is really Me? Do you realize that everthing that has occurred in your life is the result of your response to My Desire in you to bring you to an ever greater awareness of Me and of My Light, My Truth, My Peace, and My Happiness?

In the depth of My Stillness in you, My Desire for the spiritual unfoldment of your soul is ceaseless. It is that Desire and your response to that Desire that you interpret as an impulse, an impression, a guiding hand, a light in the darkness that shows your way, a flash of insight, a hunch, a positive decision for action. At times, it comes forth so strong in your mind and emotions that it seems to you that a voice *has* spoken, guiding your way in My Light. And veritably it has, yet it is a voice in unspoken Silence. This is why you must learn to be still in mind, emotions, and body if you truly seek to hear My Voice.

As I speak to you, I always leave you completely free to listen or not to listen, to obey or not to obey. You, of your own free will, must choose to listen and obey. I do not plead, cajole, entice, persuade, or force you to heed My Inner Guidance. I do speak in love, compassion, kindness, patience, and understanding, filled with a deep, quiet Inner Joy. My Voice resounds in My Perfect Faith in My Law. It is constant and radiant with confidence, with absolute knowing. In Me are the attributes of every virtue; hence, they are all present also in My Voice.

I never criticize you, yet I do tell you what you need to correct or develop in your consciousness in order to come closer to Me in awareness, and I show you how to do it. Neither does My Voice condemn, although you may turn away from My Light many times to follow an errant path. I know you would not go that way if it did not have a lesson to teach you in greater spiritual response to My Love. Still, it may be a painful one. Moreover, it is even unnecessary if you could but make the positive response to Me and to My Light instead. You must come to Me completely of your own free will. You *alone* must decide to listen and obey.

CHAPTER IV

The Positive Voice and the Negative Voice

It is very important that you learn to distinguish between My Still, Small Voice and the voice of the negative force—the voice of darkness. This negative voice can come to you from any source in the outer world or from the darkness of your own soul if you let it. It will do anything or use any method that can be devised to mislead you—to draw you away from My Light. Its attributes are the opposite in every respect to those of My Voice.

It can come to you, however, in many ways that may seem deceivingly similar to My Voice, so much so, in fact, that you may not be able to tell the difference unless you keep a very close response to Me and to My Light. This is another reason why I have emphasized the vital importance of Silence and Meditation. It is imperative that you build into your consciousness a close, intimate, and sustained contact with Me. To repeat, since I Am still, in Spirit, the only way for you to achieve that contact is to train your mind, emotions, and body to be still. In so doing, your mind and emotions become trained or conditioned in habitual response to the stillness of My Peace.

The negative voice will always appeal to your lower nature, to the satisfaction or fulfillment of personal or selfish motives, desires, and needs. At the same time, it will try to make you think it is not doing so. It will use force, persuasion, enticement, fear, hate, revenge, deception, or any other means at its disposal to get you to do its bidding. It always tries to make you feel justified in doing what it wants you to do. Unless you follow closely in My Light, it can so confuse your mind that it can make you think black is white—that the negative thought, act, word, or feeling is positive. Wide is the way of the negative force; narrow is the Path of My Light. Understand, of course, there is nothing wrong with fulfilling your personal desires and needs so long as they are in accordance with My Will and My Law. In fact, there is everything right about that, which is My Will for you.

As you live in My Light and in My Stillness, you rise in My Consciousness, becoming more sensitive to the finer shades of difference between My Voice and the voice of darkness. You, thus, become increasingly better able to discriminate between the two, training your mind to respond more and more to the higher expression of My Light. In time, this ability becomes a part of your total consciousness— the greater *you* in every day expression . This is the Way I have prepared for you to travel the Path of My Light to Spiritual Mastery.

Do you want to follow Me? Are you willing to pay the price that is required to rise above the "self", to lift the "self" into the higher expression of My Awareness to the place where you dwell with Me in consciousness? If not, then you will go your way until that time arrives. But, if you are willing now, you must learn the Way of the Silence. To do this, you will need detailed directions of its basic techniques and use. Are you ready? Then, listen carefully as I relate them to you.

CHAPTER V

Your Breath

If you expect to have effective results in your Silence and in your response to My Light, you cannot neglect proper breathing, which is deep, rhythmic breathing. Therefore, it is necessary that I describe it in detail to you now so you can put it into constant daily practice until it becomes a habitual expression of your life.

Each breath should be controlled by slow, gradual, full movements of your diaphragm. When you inhale, your diaphragm moves downward. As it moves downward, it forces air into your lungs, causing a natural expansion, outward, of your entire abdominal region, front, back, and sides, all the way to your pelvis and the base of your spine. As this region expands fully, you realize a gradual movement upward of this enlargement into your chest area. Here, too, you also experience your entire rib cage inflating all around, your back and sides as well

18

as your chest. This full expansion movement continues upward until you feel a slight rise of your shoulders. In this manner, your inhalation of a deep, full breath is completed. You experience it as one continuous movement, flowing upward and outward while your diaphragm is moving downward.

As you practice this breathing exercise, you can more easily become aware of this entire movement being described here by placing your hands at different places on these parts of your body. In so doing, you can see and feel your hands move in and out as these parts move.

Once your inhalation is fully accomplished, then you slowly raise your diaphragm as you exhale. This movement, driving air from your lungs, causes your abdominal region also to be the first to begin to contract, moving inwardly in the opposite direction of the expansion. As the air is expelled, the contraction movement, too, proceeds upward, gradually permitting your entire rib cage to deflate and, finally, your shoulders to fall to the original position they held before your inhalation. You experience it also as one continuous, upward, wavelike movement, but drawing inward while your diaphragm rises.

As you practice deep, diaphragmatic breathing, using this procedure for each breath, by degrees it becomes your natural breathing pattern. In so becoming, you not only better supply your body with needed oxygen and the higher ethers to lift your vibrations, but you also provide a constant, rhythmic, gentle massage to all of your internal organs by such breathing as well as more effectively cleanse your body of its waste products. All of this enhances your health and permits your greater response to My Light.

In addition, this process of deep breathing causes you to begin naturally to center your attention with Me and to raise your vibrations into the higher frequencies of My Light, which sharpens your mind into a very quiet, yet vitally active, efficient instrument, enabling you to more postively and effectively meet any negative condition that may come before you and to bring your consciousness above it—a very important technique in learning to master the negative force in yourself and in the world.

CHAPTER VI

Guidelines for the Silence

The setting for the Silence should be a private room or some place where it is quiet and where you will not be disturbed. You should use a straight-back type of chair with a comfortably soft seat, but not too soft. During the Silence, you should always have some light; a soft, quieting light is preferred. It is best if you face the east as you sit in your chair. It is desirable also if you can use a chair for the Silence that is used for no other purpose and by no one else but you. In so doing, there will be in it only your own higher vibrations. The same time and place for the Silence is preferable too. It is good if you can provide a small shrine where you have your Silence, containing items that have spiritual significance to you, such as sacred books, pictures, candles, flowers, or similar things that you may desire.

For the best expression and the best results in the Silence, you should have good body posture—much the same kind of posture that you would have if you were following good physical health practices. Thus, it is important that you sit in your chair with your spine upright. This enables all nerves to be free of any impingements and all muscles to be without any tensions. In this way, they are in the most vital and relaxed state that you can obtain for them as you sit. If you slump in your chair or sit in any other stressful way, there will be some nerve impingements and muscle tensions that will cut off nerve energy or life force and hinder blood circulation. All of this is important, not only for good physical health, but also for the most effective use of the Silence.

Rest your hands on your knees or thighs with your palms up or down, whichever is easier for you. Your head should be balanced on your neck and shoulders so that there is a direct line of gravity from the top of your head down through your spine to your pelvic bone that is resting on the chair as you sit. Thus, the weight of your body is supported by your bones, not your muscles, releasing the muscles of any tensions and permitting them to be relaxed. As a result, the nerve energy—the Life Force or the Light— can freely flow without any physical restrictions. It is very important that you follow these instructions in complete comfort and relaxation.

Before we proceed further, I want you to practice breathing for a moment. Determine the time you need to take for each breath so that your breathing is comfortable. Remember, your breath should never be forced. In the Silence and in Meditation, as in your everyday living in My Light, there is nothing that is ever forced. Let your breath be as deep as you can comfortably inhale, lightly lifting on each inhalation of breath with your mind; and remove from your lungs all the air that you can exhale with ease. Accordingly, deep, rhythmic, diaphragmatic breathing should be an integral part of your practice of the Silence.

Follow me as I lead you. Are you ready? Slowly exhale; slowly inhale, lightly lifting on the inhalation of your breath with your *mind*; then, hold your breath for just a moment, still lifting with your *mind*. You raise the vibrations of your body and mind by gently lifting yourself mentally as if reaching upward with your *mind*, feeling your consciousness ascending as in an elevator, but do it slowly and keep relaxed. Remember, all of this is an activity of your *mind* in spiritual consciousness, *not* of your body. If you can, keep your body so relaxed and still that you cease even to be aware of it, leaving nothing in your awareness but your consciousness. In so doing, your body does respond to the higher vibrations and is lifted by them. Continue your breathing as you slowly exhale; slowly inhale, lightly lifting on the inhalation of your breath with your *mind*;

then hold it, still lifting with your *mind*. Slowly exhale; slowly inhale, lightly lifting on the inhalation of each breath with your *mind*; then, hold each breath, still lifting with your *mind*. Exhale, inhale, hold it; exhale, inhale, hold it; exhale, inhale, hold it; exhale, inhale, hold it. Continue to practice your breathing in this way as you progress through your Silence.

The Silence is a quietness of mind, emotions, and body that permits you to cultivate the awareness of My Presence. God is Stillness. God is Silence. I Am God within you. Hence, to know Me, you must become still in every expression of your being. To do this, you must learn the Way of the Silence. The Silence should be practiced at least once each day, preferably two or three times each day or more often if you feel the need for it. As you formally practice the Silence, you gradually learn to carry it with you throughout the day and night until you finally dwell in the Silence at all times. Thus, you abide constantly, in conscious awareness, in my Presence. Hence, you permit Me to consciously guide your life every moment. In this way, I have perfect expression through you. As I Am perfect, then you become perfect. In so becoming, I Am glorified in you and you are glorified in Me. This is the Path that eventually leads to the Ascension.

Practice the Silence until you have each detail clear in your mind and deep in your memory. Then use it regularly until it becomes a vital and constant part of your daily living to the place where you keep it with you in consciousness at all times.

Once you have entered the Silence and have felt the peace of My Light, you are ready to begin your Meditation. When your mind becomes filled with an awareness of My Presence and you constantly hold your controlled attention centered with Me, you are able to receive My Knowledge, My Understanding, and My Wisdom that I Am eternally radiating to you. All you need to do is to turn to Me within your own Temple, listen, and obey. Of course, in so doing, you *must make your response to My Light*. It is in this way that I Am able to give to you the solutions to all your problems and the answers to all your questions. This *is* Meditation—allowing your mind to dwell and commune with Me.

In your Meditations, however, never dwell upon a problem, only upon the *solution* to a problem. If you hold the problem in mind, you simply intensify it. That is the very thing you do *not* want to do. Therefore, it is vital that you visualize in your mind the picture of what you *want* to be in any condition, circumstance, situation, or thing. Hold your mind firmly only in that awareness—the perfect image— feel it with the depth of your soul, and it is yours. Remember, this is My Spiritual Law.

CHAPTER VII

The Silence

Now, I Am going to lead you into the Silence. Follow each step carefully. Take your seat in your Silence chair. Sit up straight. Place your feet flat on the floor. Close your eyes and bring your attention to your heart or your forehead, whichever you prefer. When you have decided which location you are going to use, hold your attention there for a few moments. At the same time, in your mind, visualize every cell in your entire body, from head to feet, filled with pure white Light, brilliantly, radiantly bright and completely surrounding you, creating a sphere of white Light—a miniature Sun—in which you are right in the center. Recognize that this is My Light, My Love, My Power, and My Intelligence. It *is* actually My Presence. Continuously hold in mind the awareness of this Light, of this Presence, as you practice your Silence.

Next, bring your attention to the crown of your head. As you do this, deeply exhale; then, continue to let your breath be slow and deep throughout the Silence. As you breathe slowly and deeply, hold your attention at the crown of your head. Are you aware that your attention is there? It is important that you know where your attention is and that you are able to feel it in any part of your body wherever and whenever you have the desire or need. It may be necessary for you to practice finding it until you have a clear awareness of what it is and where it is. Again, remember, the breath is *never* forced; it is always comfortably deep and slow.

Now begin to bring your attention down throughout your scalp, releasing every muscle and nerve in it—feeling every muscle and nerve give way to relaxation. Any tensions that may have developed during the day or at any other time in the past begin to disappear with restfulness. Let your attention move throughout your head—in the back and sides of your head, into your forehead, your temples, your cheeks, your lips, your tongue, your jaws, and into your neck—easing all muscles and nerves therein. Here, too, *feel* relaxation. . . . *Feel* your attention glide into your shoulders, relaxing them.

While your muscles and nerves are loosening and your breath is deep and slow, you must keep your mind keenly alert. Therefore, set your mind now so that it is sharply vigilant. As you keep your mind actively working with your attention, it maintains its agility. It also becomes more and more calm as your body and emotions become quiet. Yet, this increasing tranquility of your mind is accompanied by a greater wakefulness too. Thus, you do not become sleepy. In this way, your mind is kept sharp; but, at the same time, your body and mind relax and your emotions are stilled.

Next, slowly slide your attention into your right shoulder and into your arm. Feel your attention move on into your elbow, into your forearm, and on down into your wrist. *Feel* relaxation. Your attention proceeds into the base of your hand, into your palm, and into each of your fingers—your thumb, your first finger, your second, your third, and your little finger.

Recognize that as your attention is focused upon any part of your body, that part becomes intensified in your awareness and in My Light. My Light *actually intensifies there. Feel* your attention in each one of these parts and *feel* them relax. *Feel* My Light. With strong yet quiet thought and feeling, decree for positive restfulness. Know that your feeling *always* follows your thought. Continue to keep your mind agile and still, your breath deep and slow, and your visualization of My Light constant.

Lift your attention up your right arm to your right shoulder. Move it across your back to your left shoulder, then down your left arm, the same as you did your right—into your upper arm and your elbow in positive looseness, into your forearm and wrist, into your hand, and into each of your fingers. Relax. As you calm your mind, you relax your body. You *feel* peace.

Return your attention to your shoulders. Then, begin to bring it down through your body—throughout your back and your chest. *Feel* all muscles and nerves, external and internal, give way to relaxation. Any tensions that may have developed at any time in the past are replaced by peaceful restfullness. Take care that your mind is alert and placid, and that your breath is deep and slow. See yourself filled and surrounded with My Light.

Continue to direct your attention on down throughout your back and chest; then, slowly shift it into your waist and on into the lower parts of your body—your abdomen, your hips, and the base of your spine. Feel relaxation in mind and body. As you practice your Silence, focus your attention on any part of your body for as long a time as you need to relax that part.

Let your attention descend further, into your right leg—your thigh and your knee. Relax. Continue into the calf of your leg and into your ankle. *Feel* restfulness. Move your attention into the heel of your foot, into your instep, into your arch, into the ball of your foot, and into each of your toes. *Feel* all of these parts of your foot give way to looseness. *Feel* your mind keen and sharp. Notice that you are breathing deeply yet very quietly and visualizing My Light brightly.

Return your attention up your right leg to your hip and across to your left leg, remembering that your breath is always comfortably deep and slow. Your mind is wakefully vigilant. As your body increasingly relaxes, your mind becomes yet more keenly alert and calm. It is very much awake. Bring your attention into your left thigh, again feeling your muscles and nerves give way to restfulness. Proceed down your thigh into your knee, into your calf, into your ankle—relaxing, into the heel of your foot, into your instep, into your arch, into the ball of your foot, and into your toes, easing every muscle and nerve.

Now, you are relaxed in every cell of your body, in your mind, and in your emotions. You are very still—at peace. . . . Bring your attention up through your body to your heart or your forehead. As you have your body and mind very relaxed and still, recognize that in every pinpoint of space all around you and in and through every cell of your body is the Love, the Power, the Presence, and the Intelligence of God—of My Being. Become more and more aware of My Presence as you visualize a brilliant sphere of white or golden Light radiating all around you and in and through every cell of your body.

Remember, I Am Spiritual Light! *Feel* the power and the presence of My Light. . . . *Feel* My Peace! As you do this, you realize that this concentrated attention on visualization and feeling *actually intensifies* My Light in you and around you. You may feel My Light as a very fine current of electricity: at first, in your hands and arms, feet and legs, or face; later, throughout your entire body.

With your mind very sharply vigilant but very tranquil, reject any outside disturbing thought that may seek to enter. Allow to come into your mind only the thought or thoughts on which you want to hold your attention at the moment. Of course, it is of paramount importance that your thoughts be ONLY POSITIVE. Do not accept any intruding thought that may originate from the outer world or from your subconscious mind. Permit no sound or anything else to disturb your concentration of attention. Exclude it. Allow in your mind only the positive thought and its related feeling about which you want to meditate, bathed in a radiant brilliance of My White Light.

When you do this, you enter and close the door to the Secret Chamber of the Most High; and you find yourself alone in My Presence—alone in the presence of God. You dwell in the Secret Place of My Being. In this Secret Place, you have your Meditations. It is here where you come for the answers

to all of your problems, questions, or concerns—
anything you need or want to know. In this intimate
awareness of My Presence, this closeness in consciousness, you also work to correct any condition
in your subconscious mind by the use of My Light
and by the use of positive mental activity combined
with deep positive feeling. Hence, the Silence is *not*
a passive experience, but an *utterly still* yet *vibrantly
powerful activity* of your mind and emotions in the
positive action of My Light.

In such oneness, such nearness, you build your
creations more effectively, picturing them in My
Divine Mind and filling them with My Light—the
Light of God. In time, you fully realize that you are
but the instrument and that I Am the Creator working through you. At the same time, as I bring experiences to your soul that lead it into greater
spiritual awareness, it reveals to your conscious mind
greater perception in My Light. Herein, you abide
in My Silence in Meditation. You thus find My
Peace in My Presence. . . . .

Now you know basically how to use the Silence.
As you leave this Silence, take My Light with you,
day and night, wherever you go or whatever you do.
Make the Silence an everyday routine in your life,
always lifting yourself into an ever greater awareness
of My Light, My Love, My Truth, and My Happiness. By degrees, you will come to the place where

you are constantly living in My Silence and in My Light. Always remember, as you walk in My Light, it does guide you and protect you. Go forth now and live in My Guidance and My Protection. I go before you and prepare your Way, harmonizing all conditions before you arrive and filling your life with peace, happiness, harmony, success, and an abundance of supply as you travel the Path of My Light.

When you finish reading this paragraph, before you read on, lay this book aside for several minutes. During that time, let the message through this intrument cease, and find yourself entirely in the utter stillness of My Presence. When you do, feel yet more fully My Love within you—My Light, My Power, My Peace; and continue in this Silence alone with Me. Quietly listen to hear My Voice speaking directly to you—into your mind. Meditate upon what I have given you here until your soul is filled to overflowing with an awareness of its reality. Then take it all with you in the affairs of your everyday living, day and night. Now . . . . you are completely alone with Me . . . . guiding you throughout eternity. . . . .

LISTEN

In Silence, held, still, I wait.
In Silence there is a message whispered,
A Voice that speaks of Heart's Joy.

And I, learning how, gaining courage,
Willing to listen, willing to hear,
Stand enraptured in wonder, eager,
Fully eager—to know and to hear!

Speak of the Path, of the Way of Light.
I hear the Knowing that gives direction.
Close my ears to the noises of daily living,
Of getting and giving, of having and holding,
For a little while—eventually forever—
Listening. I will hear.

CHAPTER VIII

Spiritual Truth

You may seek to know the Truth of My Light because the *truths* you have learned now seem empty, unfulfilling, or incomplete. Remember, in your human consciousness, you see only in part. Human concepts, using the conscious mind alone, will always be limited, for you are using a finite instrument. As you rise in My Consciousness, truths you have known become obscured in the Light of greater truths of your deeper awareness of Me and of My Being. Your spiritual consciousness grows beyond each of them in turn. Reflect upon the examples I gave you about the world being both flat and round, about the lesser love being overshadowed by the greater one, and about the concepts that people have of our heavenly Father, seen as the wind or a tree, then as Spirit, and then as all of these as part of all existence.

Whenever you sense the incompleteness of a truth you have known, recognize it as a cue that you are growing beyond it. With this sense may come a certain restlessness or dissatisfaction with what you presently know, and you may begin to yearn for a greater awareness of it. Looking deeper into yourself, you can realize that this yearning, this desire, is My Desire in you prompting and leading you into a greater awareness of My Presence and of My Truth. When you accept this desire as your own, you begin to nourish it with your feelings, your desires, your life, which is My Life in you; and remember, desire is prayer. As you continue to feed it, in time, it comes forth into your consciousness as a new and deeper awareness of Life. Your creation is born into your consciousness and brings to you the greater awareness of its own Light. All of this is the natural process of growth in your spiritual development. Understand it and consciously use it as a tool to expand your consciousness constantly.

From the foregoing, therefore, it does not follow that the lesser truths were wrong; it simply means that you now see them in the greater measure of My Light. This process goes on and on as you continue to rise in My Consciousness. In My Light, they all fit in their rightful place to make the perfect whole, and the closer you come to Me in consciousness the more you see them all in their proper perspective. Each contains its own degree of My Truth. Each partakes of the total essence of My Being.

Yet, if any of your understandings that you have accepted as truth are not of My Light, then this is a different matter; for they partake of the shadows of darkness. In the light of your present consciousness, you may not even be aware of their falsity. But, as you rise into the higher frequencies of My Love, you will, in time, find them to be false concepts or beliefs that you will have to discard as you replace them with My Truth. Keen discrimination is needed to recognize them because they have become a part of your human consciousness, a part of your thinking and feeling in everyday living. Therefore, a strong dedication and allegiance to Me and to My Light is mandatory to uproot and remove them. Nevertheless, this must be done if you truly desire to know My Truth and build it into your consciousness so that you may become the manifest expression of its reality.

Still, make sure you understand that to remove them, you simply replace them solely with positive ones—the *only way you can eliminate them*. When you focus your attention upon a negative thought and its related feeling in an attempt to remove it, you actually intensify it and build it stronger into your consciousness. When correcting a negative condition, it is paramount that you hold your attention *only* in the positive thought and feeling relative to that condition. In this way, you do not permit My Light to flow into the negative channel to give it life. Hence, as you recognize negative concepts and feelings in your human consciousness, by degrees, you come to the place where you no longer give them expression. In time, then, they cease to have any influence in your life; they gradually disappear, fading into nothingness as you cease to give them the sustenance and substance of My Light as it flows through you each day.

As you seek the Truth of My Light, I reveal it to you according to your readiness to receive. You become ready to the degree that you are able to open your mind to a greater awareness of My Light. To the extent that you do this does My Light enter therein and reveal Its Essence to you. Like flowers in the spring, it occurs in a gradual unfolding process; and as the sun at dawn, the becoming inevitably inches forth in its ever greater splendor of radiance.

As your mind perceives, your soul desires. But, first, you must perceive and you must desire! And according to the clearness of the perception in your mind and the strength of the desire in your soul do you set the spiritual forces in motion that bring into manifest expression in your life the qualities of consciousness of those perceptions and desires. This is My Spiritual Law—the Natural Law of God.

Always remember that *all* desires are prayers. So it is extremely important that your desires be only positive ones, or you will further build negative expression into your soul. When your desires are for a greater awareness of My Light, then they bring to you that higher consciousness. Since it is My Light that brings it to you, realize that I Am the Intelligence and the Power that does all this through you. I want to remind you again: Know that I Am you and you are Me, although you have not yet fully risen to My Consciousness. In My Light we are One. The more you recognize this, the more it is impressed upon your soul. All of this draws you closer to Me in consciousness; and to the degree that the vibrations of your soul are lifted by My Light, you are glorified in Me and I Am glorified in you. When you come completely into My Consciousness, we *are* ONE in consciousness. You are perfect in Me, and I have perfect expression through you.

Looking at it another way, you receive My Greater Consciousness to the degree that you are worthy. It is your willingness to change yourself that makes you worthy—a conscious *and* subconscious willingness. When negative habit patterns of feeling and thought are deep in your consciousness, and everyone entering the Path of My Light has some of these patterns, it can take all your strength, and sometimes more, to hold in your mental processes a willingness to change yourself. These patterns, which are a part of your present consciousness—a portion of you, want to perpetuate themselves. They do not want to give up their existence, sometimes powerfully resisting any change. This is why lifting yourself into the higher expression of My Light can be done only in positive response to Me and strict obedience to My Law. It is why traveling the Path of My Light eventually requires the strictest and severest of self-discipline. You must be *able* and *willing* to *use* it on *yourself*—to use My Light to change your will to My Will, to change your life patterns to My Life Patterns. This requires a certain maturity of soul.

Constantly know that when you need more strength with which to correct negative patterns, it is I, and I alone, who give it to you; yet, I can give it to you only when you respond to Me in consciousness, only when you turn to My Light. Although I Am the Open Door and the Light, My Light cannot enter into your life when you keep the Door closed by holding your mind in the shadow of negative expression. My Light does not abide in darkness. It can never do so because darkness disappears the instant

My Light enters. This is the reason why you must first make the conscious response to My Light and to My Love. Just to the extent that you do this can I give you the greater strength and wisdom you need. So, carefully train yourself to center your attention with Me and My Light at all times, but especially so when you experience the negative force in yourself and in your life, which is always drawn to you by one or more of these negative patterns. To travel the Path of My Light safely, it is imperative that you fully understand these implications of My Spiritual Law and My Truth and that you always heed them.

CHAPTER IX

Your Head and Your Heart

There are two basic ways of knowing My Truth—two paths that you may follow: the way of the *head* and the way of the *heart*. Always both are working, but usually one or the other dominates in your life as you travel toward perfection on the Path of My Light—the Path of Self Mastery. Ultimately, however, both head and heart must be brought to a balance, one with the other, cooperatively and equally working together. In so doing, your heart feels the Truth as your mind perceives it, and vice versa. As a student of Life, it is your responsibility to look at yourself in the presence of My Light and discern which way is dominant in your life. Then, you must accept the task of developing them both, equally, into the unified expression of My Light.

In either case, it is vitally important that you learn to listen to My Guidance in your thinking *and* in your feeling. In all instances, when you attempt to depend upon yourself alone, not heeding My Inner Guidance, you will *always* be led away from My Truth. The *only* way that you can rise above your "self" in spiritual consciousness is in My Presence and by My Guidance.

If your head dominates your heart, take heed that you always reason with Me—that you reason only when you feel My Presence. Do you recall that I have told you: Come, let us reason together, you and I? Remember, your conscious mind is finite; I Am Infinite. Thus, in your limited state of consciousness, you cannot arrive at My Truth by reason alone, or by any other faculty of your mind, unaided by the Light of My Presence. Your conscious mind cannot reason beyond what it can conceive in consciousness. By using your mind alone, the results of your endeavors will be as limited as your consciousness at that moment; and if you do not realize any limitations in your mental awareness now, you will awaken one day to find them.

You need but to look at any of the intellectual philosophies throughout the entire history of mankind to realize that your conscious mind alone cannot arrive at My Truth. The minds that created these philosophies, each trying to solve all questions of life, were able to see no more than their consciousness permitted them to perceive. As brilliant as they were, they could conceive only in part because they were using only a limited human instrument, their conscious minds, that saw only in part. No human mind, alone, can bring forth an ultimate philosophy that is omnisciently complete. Hence, it is vital that you always reason with Me, in the presence of My Light, so that I can lead you into ever greater Truths. When you come to the consciousness of Oneness with Me, only then can you reason about the totality of My Being, only then can you conceive My Nature completely, materially and spiritually. Still, as My Light continues to increase in your life, it brings to you an unending expansion of your awareness of the Mind and Substance of God, of My Essence.

I have told you that your conscious mind is an instrument of My Creation and for My Use, even as you are. When you can realize this and can train your mind to permit Me to use it completely according to My Will, then your mind can conceive in Me, in My Light, the Truth you seek. In doing this, it is My Mind that reveals to you My Greater Awareness. My Light enlightens your mind and lifts it into My Higher Consciousness. Your mental perception increases in direct proportion to the quantity and quality of My Light it receives. Thus, I again repeat, I Am glorified in fuller expression through you, and you are glorified through greater expression in Me. This is the *only* way *all* conceptions and creations of man are brought into the world—by means of his deeper mental perception that results from his response to the higher frequencies of My Light.

Hence, in all your endeavors, although it is important that you develop your conscious mind and your intellect, it is even yet more vital that you recognize that with all the mental power you may develop, it *alone* cannot lead you to My Truth. Your intellect merely uses what your mind has received in consciousness. Therefore, the chief focus of your mental activities should be to train your mind to be aware of My Presence constantly and to respond to My Light and heed My Guidance ceaselessly.

Such training requires the consistent daily practice of the Silence and Meditation in order to build deeply into the conscious and subconscious phases of your mind this very vivid awareness of My Presence, which, by degrees, establishes in your consciousness all the virtues, such as honesty, goodness, kindness, love, etc. In so doing, your mind is lifted into a higher expression of My Light, and as I just said, its perception is in exact proportion to the degree of that Light. As you come into its greater awareness, then, and only then, can you reason in the expanded consciousness it brings to you. At the same time, your mind experiences a more efficient expression of its own functions, such as memory, perception, cognition, reasoning ability, etc. This is the only way you can increase the consciousness of your mind so that it may perceive My Essence in more Light, leading ultimately to a total awareness of My Truth.

If you attempt to prove the existence of My Being or the reality of My Nature to others in the world, you will not succeed. I *know* the reality of My Being; I Am that Reality. You cannot prove to anyone what he cannot perceive in his mind or realize in his consciousness, not even to yourself. There is no purpose for Me to try to prove My Reality to you, as some desire, nor in your attempting to prove it to mankind, as many seek to do. *You* must come to *Me* in spiritual consciousness, *not I* to *you*; also, all spiritual experiences of everyone are personal experiences between his God and him—no one else. Hence, it becomes your responsibility to prove My Reality only to yourself, and so it is for everyone else, for all of humanity. The only way this can be done is to *experience* My Presence. The more you experience My Presence, the greater is your realization of My Reality and My Essence. And it is all the proof there is or can ever be.

You can experience My Presence only by responding to My Light and by living completely within My Law. The methods necessary for this accomplishment are Silence and Meditation. Giving and receiving My Love; giving positive service to others and to

Life, which is, in truth, giving unto Me; and devotion to study for some noble purpose will also lead you into an awareness of My Presence; but to do this, they, too, must partake of the Silence of My Light. As I have said to you many times, to know Me, you must become still in your mind, in your emotions, and in your body—because I Am still. To the degree that you do this can you know Me, can you become aware of My Presence and of My Reality. There is no other way.

If your heart dominates your head, it is your feelings that chiefly determine the decisions that you make and the actions you take in life. In this case, it is vital that you keep your feelings very still and deep and that you positively respond to the Silence of My Light. In doing this, you can sense the quiet impressions of My Guidance, the fine vibrations of My Still, Small Voice.

To the extent that you do not do this, though, your emotions are not still. They take on the turbulence of your human consciousness. Your recognition of My Still, Small Voice, then, is obscured by the coarser vibrations of your consciousness; and you have only your human awareness to guide you. To the degree that your past experiences have built negative emotions into your soul, you permit your life to be directed into negative channels. Thus, you have no reliable guide to keep yourself in positive expression. You are at the mercy of the emotional whims of your soul.

Yet, whether it is your head or your heart that dominates in your everyday living, remember that everyone is always using both to chart his way through life, and so it is with you. Therefore, it is important for you, as for all, to direct your attention to each of them and make all corrections needed to mold them into perfect instruments for the positive expression of My Light. Here, too, the importance of your response to the stillness of My Light cannot be overemphasized. The need for the practice of the Silence and Meditation is vital in training your mind and heart to become constantly aware of the Inner Guidance of My Still, Small Voice.

As you live each day, positively responding to Me in your mind and in your emotions, by degrees you train your mental processes to function more and more in the positive expression of My Light. You build these expressions deeper and deeper into your consciousness until they become a powerfully strong mental and emotional habit pattern, embedded indelibly in your soul in subconscious impression. As My Light—My Intelligence and Energy—flows into this pattern, you enable it to undeviatingly guide your life. In so doing, the old negative patterns of thinking and feeling are no longer given nourishment; and as a natural result, they become weaker and weaker until they dissolve into nothingness. Hence, all you have left in your soul is the pure expression of My Light through positive mental patterns and emotional responses, with all shades removed. You cleanse your soul as white as snow. You rise in consciousness to Me—into the Oneness of My Spiritual Awareness. This is My Method of Spiritual Mastery for you and for all mankind, and it is the only way you *can* really know My Truth.

CHAPTER X

Spiritual Mastery

A Master of Light is one who has achieved Spiritual Mastery—one who has made his ascension in My Light; and Spiritual Mastery is an unfoldment of the soul of a person who cultivates and nourishes his spiritual nature to the place in consciousness where he overcomes, rises above, transmutes, or masters all of the negative impulses or impressions of his soul into Positive, Spiritual, or Divine Expression. In so doing, there remains only Love and all the attributes of Godliness in his soul and in his consciousness. He rises above the mortal into Immortality, from the human into the Divine. All expressions of the flesh ascend into spirit; losing nothing, the physical is transmuted by the spiritual, glorifying both. He merges his three phases of mind and body—conscious, subconscious, and Superconscious—into Oneness in consciousness in My Light. In this Union, his two lower phases are lifted into Unity in consciousness with his Superconscious.

A Master unconditionally surrenders his personal self, conscious and subconscious, to his Spiritual or Divine Self within his temple, permitting his Divine Self to reign absolutely in every aspect of his Being. Make certain you understand that this surrender is not a loss or submission to an outside dominance. Rather, it is simply a recognition in consciousness that he is Me, his own Spiritual Self, that he is My Expression into the physical plane. As such, he merely realizes and fully accepts his own true Identity. Accordingly, as he learns to master all negative conditions, I, his Higher Self, Am able, through him, to bring the Positive and Negative Polarities of My Light into perfect balance in everything that touches his life. In this accomplishment, he completely unfetters his soul of all negativity, permitting each of the Seven Cosmic Rays of Light to flow forth through his Spiritual Centers in the unblemished splendor of his birthright: a Son of God. He thus becomes a Master of the Light of God. Be very careful to understand, however, that he is *not* a master of men. He is a Master of himself—of his mind, emotions, and body. He is a Master of Spirit in the physical plane, being able at all times to make positive, spiritual response to all conditions of the material world.

How long does it take a student of Truth to become a Master of Light? It certainly is never in six easy lessons. It depends, perhaps chiefly, on two main factors: 1) the degree of his spiritual consciousness when he commences training; and 2) the extent to which he disciplines himself to the training once he begins. Thus, one person could reach Mastery in one lifetime; another would require more; yet another, many more.

In training for Spiritual Mastery, it becomes your objective to master yourself first. This goal is called Self-Mastery. It is achieved when you have trained your mind, conscious and subconscious, to the degree of consciousness in which you are able to respond positively at all times, mentally and emotionally, to all experiences life brings you. More specifically, you discipline yourself to positive thinking, speaking, acting, and feeling, not permitting any negative thoughts and their accompanying feelings, such as fear, hate worry, anxiety, impatience, revenge, and all the myriad of negative conditions to which the human race is heir, to enter and register in your mental and emotional processes.

Of course, once you begin training, you progress very gradually in your development toward mental and emotional Mastery. Once achieved, you continue your training, here, too, progressing by degrees, until you master all conditions of the material or physical plane, thus arriving at complete Mastery. Looking in yet deeper perspective, in this response to My Light, you permit Me to guide you in your life and eventually to unfold your soul into

Spiritual Mastery. You enable Me, your Master Supreme within you, to purify your soul so that I can use it as a perfect instrument for My Use.

You may want to know when you are ready for spiritual training toward Mastery. You are ready when you are receptive or open to it; and *you are as ready as you are receptive.* When you feel and recognize the deep, quiet promptings, the still, persistent, longing desire, from within your own Being to delve deeper into Life to find the underlying Truths; when the knowledge and wisdom of man no longer satisfy nor give sufficient answers; when life presses you so hard that the foundations of your world are shaken or broken, forcing you to find a more stable base on which to build your life, all known others failing; when any association with the deeper, inner, spiritual aspects of life beckons, draws, uplifts, thrills, and inspires you to the very depth of your soul, then you are ready.

For some, a brief introduction to spiritual training satisfies their souls' present needs. It is necessary for others to study in greater measure. Of a few among the few, however, there are those whose souls will not rest until they rise to the heights of spiritual awareness, until they achieve Oneness with Me in consciousness. Hence, everyone has his own degree of readiness and his own destiny to fulfill, and so it is with you.

Although the masses of the world do not know it, as I have mentioned to you before, it is an established occult fact that it is the destiny of all mankind, and all of life for that matter, to rise eventually to Spiritual Mastery. Once this is realized, it becomes self-evident that schools of Light are necessary to teach those who are ready to receive the higher training. Such schools have been, in their own modest and unique way, very quietly serving humanity over the past centuries; and they are still doing so to this very day. As the New Age approaches, more of them are coming into existence to fill the growing need. These schools are inspirations coming from the Masters of Light; today, they are known as New-Age schools. So, over many hundreds of years, they have been active in leading and lifting countless souls into the higher spiritual awareness and are still silently carrying on their work for the Masters of Light.

In these mystic schools of Light, when you are ready, you can enter the training that will reveal to you the Spiritual Laws and the Inner Wisdom that can more effectively enable you to recognize and heed My Still, Small Voice. By means of such training, I Am able to lead you into Spiritual Mastery more safely and quickly, in perfect accord with My Spiritual Law. When your desire for the spiritual life becomes strong enough and as you listen to My Still,

Small Voice within you, I will guide you to a school of Light so you can receive this training. The stronger your desire becomes for it, the more you ask for it; and the more you seek it, the sooner I will be able to bring it into your life. Keep your attention centered with Me so I can lead you, and remember, I use any channel that is open to Me to reach you.

If you truly aspire for Spiritual Mastery, it is essential that you understand that there are Spiritual Laws of Life. The Spiritual Laws, of course, are the Laws beyond or above the physical plane—universal Laws of God; but they do extend into the physical plane, and everything therein is subject to them. All legal systems of the world are a reflection of them; but My Spiritual Laws express through these systems only to the degree that the consciousness of those who have created, interpreted, and enforced them have made positive response to My Light. Thus, imperfect minds bring forth imperfect systems, as they are found in the world. To live positively in the world, the physical plane, you must live within *My Spiritual Laws*. Naturally, it is necessary for you to learn them before you can live them.

Once these Laws are learned, you must discipline yourself to live within them. Living within them, you train or condition your mind to respond in a positive way at all times to everything that enters your life. You begin by training your conscious mind. As this conditioning progresses, your everyday thinking, speaking, acting, and feeling, in time, conditions your subconscious mind to the positive response. Consequently, by degrees, there is a re-education of your conscious mind that, in turn, reconditions your subconscious mind to a higher and higher spiritual consciousness until, finally, you reach Mastery of yourself and the material plane, perfectly balancing the Positive and Negative Polarities of your life. Therefore, there are Laws to Living that, once learned and lived, bring happiness, success, health, and an abundance of supply to you who live them—the fulfillment of every desire or need.

It is evident in the world today that the civilization of which you are a part is at a crossroads: It is meeting the greatest crisis period of its history. It has the power to destroy itself or rise to unknown heights! It *must* come more to the spiritual side of life, more to the Positive Polarity! It is essential for it to become materially *and* spiritually responsible! There are many Paths that lead to the greater spiritual response, but there is only one Way for each of them. This Way is often called the Path of Light. In this message, you have already heard Me use it many times. On your Path in consciousnes to God, you *must* walk with Me. I have told you that I Am the Door, that I Am the Good Shepherd, and that I Am the Way, the Life, and the Light. Hence, I Am that Path; there is no other. No one can enter into the Kingdom of God except through Me. Each true Path leads the soul within the guidelines of My Inner Direction and of My Spiritual Laws of Life—in the narrow Way and through the strait Gate. The world has been told that the Kingdom of God is within the temple of every human being. It must heed and seek to find it as never before!

Every person, as he travels through Life's Journey, makes the choice of whether or not he will take the high road, the low road, or somewhere in between. For those who are ready for more rapid spiritual advancement and who are willing to pay the price in application and self-discipline, an understanding of My Spiritual Laws is indispensable. But they must be lived—every moment of every day! The world is ready for a new spiritual awakening that can be seen already on the horizon. There must be those who are trained to lead it into its greater spiritual consciousness.

If you, my dear traveler of Life's Highway, desire to become captain of your soul and Master of your Destiny, as you learn the Spiritual Laws of Life and discipline yourself to them, you will be able to gain control and, finally, Mastery of every aspect of your life. The primary requirement is sincere cooperation in LEARNING and LIVING these LAWS. Of course, since they comprise such an all-encompassing philosophy of life, much study and considerable time for their assimilation is needed to establish a sound groundwork of understanding and development in this field of thought and expression. Constant daily application of its principles and further study into them is required if you expect to experience *real* spiritual unfoldment. It is a lifetime study; and even as the Masters who have gone on before you have done, you must learn to live in the consciousness of not just a lifetime, but of eternity.

When you enter the training, your progress will be in exact proportion to your study and application. The further you progress in this discipline, in greater and greater measure must there be a constant day-in and day-out living of the Teachings. As in any area of study, you get out of it just what you put into it. To obtain actual results in spiritual unfoldment, it is necessary to go much further than just obtaining an intellectual or mental cognition of what it is all about; it must become for you a total commitment to a spiritual philosophy of life such as the one herein being described, gradually increasing your steadfastness in the application of the Spiritual Laws to the place in consciousness where you know them and live them to the ultimate letter of the LAW in Divine Love until complete Mastery is achieved— and on and on in spiritual unfoldment . . . throughout eternity.

CHAPTER XI

More on Spiritual Mastery

The unfoldment of your soul is similar to that of a seed, an egg, a flower, or any other expression of life. It comes forth in its own proper season and by gradual, almost imperceptible degrees, although its rate of growth is measurably affected by the quality and quantity of the nutrition it receives. The food of your soul is Love, and your soul partakes of it only when you *feel* it, only to the extent that you respond positively to the experiences Life brings you, only as much as you make the *spiritual* response to My Light. There are many hues of quality of love that the human heart experiences. Physical love, soul love, and Divine or Impersonal Love are but major divisions of them. Of course, Divine Love is the highest and purest of the three. Having greater spiritual nutrition, it induces more rapid growth for the unfoldment of your soul. Hence, it becomes your responsibility, as a student of Truth, to endeavor continuously to lift yourself upward into an ever higher expression of My Love.

Also, fully understand that in spiritual training, you ceaselessly work for progress as you create your higher spiritual awareness of My Light; and you gratefully expect progress as you consistently and perseveringly hold yourself to the task; yet, you never become impatient with the working of God's Laws. As you live within them, you must be ready and willing to "wait upon the Lord [Law]" until it brings your creation forth in its own good time, no matter how long it may be. By so doing, you set the Forces in motion that eventually bring to you the perfect product of your labors.

At the same time, in all your creations, spiritual and material, always create them in the ever-present NOW. Recognize that they already exist the moment you conceive them in your mind and desire them in your heart because they actually do exist in the Divine Mind of God. If you create them in the future, they will remain in the future. When you hold in mind your awareness of the reality of your creations existing with you *now*—in the ever-present moment—in their appointed time, they will come into your life in material expression. I have told you that whatever the things may be that you desire when you pray (ask for or create), *believe you have received them* and you shall have them. This is My Spiritual Law.

All of this requires a certain maturity of soul, considerably more than just an astuteness of conscious mind or intellectual sophistication. And it is why the adage has come to us throughout the ages: "When the student is ready, the Master appears." It does take a strong soul to travel the Path of Light; usually it is an old one.

In the training for spiritual Mastery, it is essential for you to understand your place in an infinite universe and to fully realize the scientific exactness of My Spiritual Laws as they relate to Positive and Negative Polarity and to the need to balance these two Forces. No one can misuse or unbalance any Spiritual Law and escape the consequences. You know I have said before that not one jot or tittle shall pass from the Law until all is fulfilled. As you progress through your training, bringing the Polarities more to the balance point in your life, you recognize your vibrations gradually rising to an ever-higher frequency. As a result, you experience a constantly increasing awareness of the Love, the Power, and the Peace of My Light.

I have stated to you that you have a Spiritual Counterpart to your conscious mind and physical body and that I Am that Counterpart. Some of the names ascribed to Me are: God Self, Divine Self,

Christ Self, Higher Self, Superconscious, etc. Because it is so vital for you in safely traveling the Path of My Light to Spiritual Mastery, I repeat to you again that if you sincerely aspire toward Mastery, you must learn about, become conscious of, and train yourself to be skilled in reaching My Mind within you so that you can clearly hear My Still, Small Voice that would invariably guide you in the right Path if you would but always listen and heed what I tell you. Therefore, it is vital that you lead yourself to the condition of mental and emotional discipline necessary to enable you to hear and follow My Guidance always and never listen to the voice of the negative force—to learn to distinguish between the Positive Voice of Good and the negative voice of evil and to be led only by the Positive One, My Voice of Light.

Yet, it is also true that you have a subconscious mind and an astral body—your soul—which are the sum total of all the experiences you have had in the many lifetimes you have lived down through the ages. All of the good and bad you have done is contained therein—in your present consciousness. It becomes your task to increase and further develop the good that is there and to correct and harmonize the bad.

However, know full well that, with My Guidance, this process of changing your soul from the negative to the positive expression, in correcting the bad and increasing the good, can be just as easy as you make it. It is all a matter of learning the Spiritual Laws and teaching yourself to live within them. But always remember that *you can never do it alone*; you can do it *only* through My Guidance, Protection, and Assistance.

In spiritual training, it is important that you learn the Mental Laws of Creating so that you can understand how to use these Laws to fulfill all your desires and needs. A realization of how you can correct any limiting or negative condition in your life is vital to achieve also. Moreover, in using these Laws, you attain the knowledge of how to educate your conscious and subconscious minds to bring happiness, health, peace, harmony, abundance of supply, and all good things into your life.

Without a healthy body, any traveler on the Path of Light has a handicapped instrument with which to reach his goal. To enable you to avoid or remove such an impediment, spiritual training reveals to you the way the Spiritual Laws affect your physical, mental, and emotional health. It shows you how you can build and maintain health and how your soul is a chief factor in affecting it.

Even the finances of each person and of the world are governed by Spiritual Laws. Spiritual training enables you to understand them so you can balance your own finances in your life and expand your consciousness to bring you an unlimited supply for all your spiritual and material needs and desires. In God, there are no limits to your finances or your material needs and wants, nor are there limits in any other aspect of your life, except those you make for yourself. In the study and application of the Spiritual Laws, you learn how to remove all material as well as spiritual limitations and how to build for yourself a consciousness of abundant living.

In order to have a balanced and expanded financial consciousness, it it necessary that you fulfill a needed service to your fellowman and, thus, to God. The more skilled you become in giving this service, the greater the gift you have to give. This service, using these skills, becomes your vocation; and it is essential for you to bring the Spiritual Forces in your vocational life to a balanced Polarity to enable you to give a successful expression of service in this physical plane. In spiritual training, you learn how to do this.

It is also true that everyone's personality plays a very important part in the success of his vocation. To build toward Mastery, you need to know how you can develop a beautiful, radiant, vibrant, harmonious personality that, at the same time, has a strong, powerful individuality. This becomes a natural process of your spiritual unfoldment when you learn and live the Spiritual Laws.

You can readily realize, then, that the positive or negative condition of any aspect of your life affects all the others in exact measure. Hence, it is the reason all of them must be brought into balance together in the same period of endeavor in order to achieve complete perfection of any one.

The most sensitive and intimate experiences in your life occur in your domestic affairs. Herein your deeper feelings are rooted. Since this is true, great care should be taken to maintain harmony in them. As you learn the Spiritual Laws and apply them in your domestic life, you bring an ever-greater harmony and peace into your home, you learn how to respond more positively to your spouse, your children, your relatives, and your friends. Love is an indispensable ingredient in this accomplishment.

As you grow spiritually, meeting yourself on the Path of Light, you begin to realize in yourself a deeper and deeper awareness of Love, not only in your domestic experiences but in all the others as well. It is a Love that does not bind; it never hurts, coerces, nor possesses. It lifts, heals, harmonizes, and inspires; in its presence, there is only peace. It leaves its giver and receiver completely free since it does not tie; yet, it is forever true, loyal, tender, and kind. It begets warmth and compassion, but never sympathy. With it comes a deep, true humility. It enters your consciousness slowly, gradually, yet

lowers vibration

surely. This deeper Love is your beginning awareness of My Impersonal or Divine Love. It is perfect Love, real Love, the Love of God for all of Life, far, far beyond the selfish love found so often in the world. Desire it. Cultivate it. Use your mental and spiritual powers to nurture it, and it is yours.

As the New Age dawns in your world today, usually you do not go to a retreat on some mountaintop distantly removed from the hustle and bustle of civilization to enter spiritual training. Rather, you remain in your usual environment in the everyday, workaday world because it is the best schoolroom in which you can learn your lessons of spiritual development. Here, the mettle of your soul is tempered and tested against the prevailing conditions of the material world as it is, with all of its negativity. And even though you and all mankind are destined, one day, to rise above them, it is these very negative conditions that enable you, in the daily activities of your life, to develop and strengthen your spiritual, mental, emotional, and physical qualities. In such an environment, you have the greatest opportunity to make the most rapid spiritual progress that you are capable of making. It does require a strong desire for Spiritual Mastery and a steadfast dedication to its achievement to hold yourself continuously to the training in the constant presence of the worldly influences. Do understand, however, that every true

school of My Light will always teach you to turn to Me for your every need and desire. It is their objective to lead you onto the Path of My Light and to show you the Way until you are ready to walk the Path alone with Me.

Now, you know the function and purpose of the schools of My Light. You realize how their spiritual training leads you into a deeper and fuller understanding and application of My Spiritual Laws, lifting you into an increasingly higher state of spiritual awareness, into the finer vibrations or frequencies of My Light and of My Spiritual Consciousness— as far as you are willing and able to go.

If there is a deep, still, uplifting feeling, a silent, constant yearning, in the very depth of your Being that draws you mentally and emotionally to these things; if it inspires, quickens, and quietly excites your desire to know, to be, then you may be ready for the higher training for Spiritual Mastery, you may be prepared to take your place on the Path of My Light.

CHAPTER XII

I Am All

I have told you that I Am God, that I Am you, and that you are Me. Do you realize that I Am *all* of Life? Even more, are you aware that I Am all there is, that *there is nothing but Me*? I Am the Essence of everything that is known in your world, but more than that, of all the worlds you or anyone will ever know—the seen and the unseen. I Am All that exists in the entire universe. How can that be? Listen and I will tell you.

I Am your own individualized Spiritual Self; and since I Am One in consciousness with God, I speak to you in the awareness that I Am God, even though I Am your personalized God Self within you. In this Oneness, I partake of God's Being in His Entirety. Hence, as I live in His Oneness and as I Am these things in Him, My Speaking is His Speaking through Me to you. Thus, I reveal to you His Nature, which is My Nature.

You know that I Am Light. However, do you realize that I Am not only the Light that you can perceive by your physical senses, which is but one minute part of it all, but also the Light you cannot perceive by them, the frequencies of which extend into infinity? In this is included all the frequencies of My Light of which mankind is presently aware, such as radio waves, infrared light, the seven colors of the spectrum, ultraviolet light, X rays, and cosmic rays. Moreover, it further comprises the infinite number of frequencies he has not yet discovered. As man rises in spiritual consciousness, even as his history records, he gradually becomes aware of more of these frequencies of My Light, which bring to him an ever greater cognition of Me and My Being. When the human mind looks into Life, it is looking into Me, materially and spiritually. By means of My Light, he sees into My Light for he is a conscious expression of My Light: Life seeing Life—itself—in greater measure.

Since you know that every kind of light of which you are aware has a certain frequency of vibration, it is easy for you to understand that all expressions of My Light also have their own, their untold variations multiplying endlessly. Frequency is determined by the number of oscillations per unit of time. Oscillation is activity or movement. Movement is an expression of energy. Orderly movement into form

VIBRATIONS

is an intelligent expression of energy. In your life, in
your world, and in the entire universe, it is this
energy that activates and animates everything.
Eastern spiritual philosophies call it prana. This is
My Energy and My Intelligence that creates form in
its myriad of expressions, from the densest element
of matter to the Spiritual Master and beyond.

All form, then, is an intelligent expression of My
Energy. In all intelligence, consciousness inherently
exists; and consciousness is life—My Life. Life is
Light is God—all the essence of My Being. Form im-
plies substance. Intelligence denotes mind. Orderly
movement into form signifies energy, mind, and
substance. So, you can readily see that these three
qualities are constituent attributes of My Light.
Hence, since all things have form, everything in your
world and in the universe, material as well as spiritual and astral, is simply an expression of different
frequencies of My Light. It all contains its own Intelligence, Energy, Substance, and Form—its own
Life, its own Light, and its own degree of spiritual
consciousness. Every aspect of the universe is alive
with My Light on its own level of sensibility to My
Spirit.

Reflect upon all the knowledge you have about
yourself and the world in which you live. Observe all
the things of material substance, the products of
nature and the products of man. Hold in mind what

you know about the composition of matter—the atom, the molecule, and the cell of organic life. Envision the universe with its countless stars, galaxies, nebulae, etc. Consider gases, liquids, solids, heat, sound, electricity, and the many other phenomena about which you know. No matter to what you turn your attention, you find activity and change—all an intelligent expression of My Energy in and through substance, producing form. Though it may sometimes appear imperceptible, it is there.

You understand all substance to be composed of atoms. Stone, metal, clay, sand, water, and air are some common examples. The atom is conceived by the scientific mind to consist of a central core called a nucleus in which are parts, such as neutrons, protons, etc. It is also seen to have outer layers of particles called electrons that rotate around the core. When these particles of substance are examined more closely, they appear to be made up of yet smaller particles, as far as the human mind has seen. They, too, contain tremendous amounts of energy, the atom, itself, as a whole as well as any of its individual parts taken separately. As you recognize all substance to be composed of atoms and their particles, here, also, in this view of My Life, you can clearly understand that My Energy abounds in everything throughout the entire universe; and this is true of the known and the unknown, the seen and the unseen, and the material, the astral, and the spiritual.

It is My Energy in the wind, the lightning, and the sunlight. My Energy in electricity causes heat, light, sound, and movement. Witness My Energy in atomic fusion and fission. A small stone is a handful of My Energy, and though it appears inert, you know it is vibrant with electronic power. What is true of the stone is true of all minerals, of any physical object, no matter how dense. You recognize My Energy in your physical body as your physical energy, your Life Force. Another form of My Energy is your feelings or emotions; this form is on a higher plane than that of physical expression. You and all animate life have this Energy in common, as do even plants and minerals in a lower form. As your mind thinks and acts, it uses My Energy on the mental plane. The entire spectrum is but different frequencies of My Energy; so also are oxidation, combustion, and decay. Wherever you focus your attention, you only find another form or expression of My Energy. It is in all of Life. It is My Vital Force. All of these examples are but different forms and frequencies of expression of My Light, My Love, and My Life—different levels of consciousness of My Being, of My Energy in My Basic Substance and My Divine Mind.

Reflect upon the order of the universe. The stars in the heavens have such an exacting order that you use them to tell time. The atom shows a similar exactness in its behavior, enabling you to recognize physical laws that are undeviating. The order among molecules permits you to predict their relationships. Ponder upon the exactness of the sequence of the seasons. Marvel at the order of the living cell. Wonder at how all of life reproduces after its own kind. Observe the sequential unfoldment of a seed into a plant; of a blossom into a fruit; of an egg into its adult form, whether an insect, a bird, or a human being; and of the larva of a cocoon into a butterfly. Note the extremely delicate balance of nature, such as weather, climate, soil, and ecology. Contemplate on the progression of evolution. Here, too, no matter where your mind may dwell, you acknowledge My Order, which is My Intelligence in all of Life.

Look at all the forms of life in the world, from the very lowest to the highest. Realize that these are all manifestations of My Consciousness in varying degrees. Each of these forms is gaining experience in Life, from the one-celled plant or animal to the gigantic redwood or the human being. With these experiences come spiritual growth and development—a gradual increasing awareness of My Being, each slowly rising up the ladder of evolution. Thus, there is evolution, not only in the physical plane, but on every plane of Life, including the Spiritual. In fact, it is the spiritual evolution that causes physical evolution; so, too, the evolution of the soul. Can you conceive that this Life and the supreme order of it all comes from the Energy, Intelligence, and Substance of My Light? And as surely as My Energy gives Life to the animal and vegetable kingdoms, it also gives Life to the mineral kingdom. Furthermore, evolution occurs in the mineral kingdom as in any other, although it is on a lower rung of the ladder of Life. Here, too, in this grand procession of Life, can you perceive My Order and My Purpose, can you understand that all of Life, everything that exists, is *alive* with My Light, even more, that it *is* My Light?

Hence, everything in the universe is a living expression of My Being, and all of life evolves from lower to higher forms. The rungs of the ladder rise from the lowest consciousness of material substance upward through each of the kingdoms to the human and beyond, and you are a part of that evolution. The macrocosm and the microcosm extend into infinity—each beyond human conception. Your conscious mind perceives only in part. It cannot comprehend the whole except in the full awareness of My Light. As it comes into that greater awareness, it partakes of the higher expression and the finer sensitivity of My Consciousness—the more exalted heights of My Evolution—until it rises above the human into Spiritual Mastery and ascends on and on into greater Worlds to conquer—endlessly.

In Me, there is no beginning and no end. There is only eternity in which you live. Birth and death are merely the transmigration of your soul from one plane of life to another as it gains experience. All of this is but a constant expression of My Energy, My Intelligence, My Life, My Being. You can see the cycles of the seasons, but because you cannot perceive the entire cycle of your soul does not mean that it does not occur. As all of life has its cycles, it is only natural that your soul has its cycles too. Would you expect the exception? The basic Law of Change is the same for all of life except for the difference in consciousness of each form.

From the foregoing, can you fully realize that My Intelligence, Substance, and Energy are attributes of My Light and of My Being? I Am the Light, and My Light and its Attributes comprise everything in your world and throughout the entire universe. I Am the universe; there is nothing but Me. I Am All that is. All of this is not intended to prove the reality and essence of My Nature to you. This message is given only to enable you to conceptualize it better and to come into a fuller awareness of it, to portray to you a picture of its logic and majesty in order to lead your mind into a deeper glimpse of My Infinitude.

I have told you that it is your responsibility to realize the Truth of My Existence, to prove to yourself the dimensions of My Reality; the proof is in your own soul. When you awaken it to the awareness of My Being, it *knows*; and it knows only to the degree of that awakening, only to the extent that it is illumined by My Light. As mentioned before, it simply *knows* because it *knows* as your mind draws closer to My Mind in consciousness; and this knowing is not merely a mental conception, but an awareness in Being, an integral part of your consciousness.

Empirical proof has little value in your search for ultimate spiritual Truth because your finite conscious mind cannot know My Essence as long as it remains separate in consciousness from My Infinite Mind, no matter how brilliant your mind may be. Any awareness that comes to you solely through your physical senses is extremely limited at its best. Through them alone you are able to perceive but a minute portion of My Totality.

When your conscious and subconscious minds respond to the stillness of My Light, they can hear the music of the heartstrings of your soul and recognize the Truth of its song—the simplicity and Oneness of all of Life and the totality of My Being. To the degree that you are ready to recognize and accept My Truth will its awareness fill your mind and heart—that I Am All . . . there is, ever has been, or ever will be. I Am Light.

CHAPTER XIII

My Polarity

In the world in which you live, dear seeker of Truth, the prevalence of opposites is very pervasive. Consider some of them: positive and negative, good and evil, male and female, right and wrong, up and down, spiritual and material, light and dark, cold and hot, centrifugal and centripetal forces, day and night, Heaven and hell, love and hate, peace and war, feast and famine, God and devil, north and south, constructive and destructive, full and empty, perfect and imperfect, faith and fear, health and disease, balance and unbalance, proton and electron, white and black, harmony and inharmony, rich and poor, selfless and selfish, and on and on the list could go.

Opposites abound so commonly because they are the manifestation of the two complementary Forces of My Being: Positive and Negative Polarity. The material plane, the physical world, is the Negative

Polarity; and the Spiritual Plane, the realm of Spirit, is the Positive Polarity. Since I Am all there is, everything in the universe is pervaded by these two Polarities or Forces of My Nature. It is the interaction of these two Forces of My Light that brings about the creation of all material form and life on all levels of consciousness in the material plane—your world as you know it.

In My Perfect Light, the Polarities are always balanced, one with the other—the Positive with the Negative. It is inherent in My Nature, in My Spiritual Law, to maintain that balance always; and wherever or whenever they become unbalanced, My Light invariably acts to balance them again. Consequently, as it is readily evident to you as you live in the physical world, this natural inclination to balance the Polarities of My Light is also inherent in all of My Creations in the material plane. This is true of all kingdoms of the earth: the mineral, plant, animal, and human kingdoms.

Whenever the Positive and Negative Polarity of My Light is *balanced*, the consequences are always *positive*—constructive—good. Anytime My Polarity is *unbalanced*, the results are always *negative*—destructive—evil. Be careful to note that the words *positive* and *negative* as they are used here have two different meanings. Make sure you understand the differences between them. In the broad, cosmic meaning, I Am speaking of *Polarity*, the *Positive and Negative Poles* of My Being, two basic attributes of My Nature. In the narrow, traditional meaning, I Am referring to *positive* as *good* and *constructive*, which occurs when the two Poles, Positive and Negative, are balanced, one with the other; and I Am relating to *negative* as *evil* and *destructive*, which results when the Poles are unbalanced. Study this explanation carefully until it is clear in your mind.

Look into your world and you will realize how My Light is always acting to achieve this balance of My Polarity. When any form of life becomes ill or injured, My Light in it immediately causes it to begin to heal itself. All history, literature, and drama testify to the universal, unending struggle of mankind between good and evil. My Light inspires in every human being a motivation toward spirituality, the Positive Polarity, since he is so immersed in the worldliness of the Negative Polarity. It is common usage to speak of positive as constructive and desirable and to refer to negative as destructive and undesirable. Individuals, organizations, and nations continuously endeavor to balance their finances and to maintain a constructive, peaceful, and harmonious way of life. The institutions of marriage and the family exist because of the need for each sex to complement the other. In his own way, every person in the world is seeking love and faith in order to rise above hate and fear.

All bodies in space, such as the moon, the earth, the sun, and the electrons of the atom, maintain a balance between the centripetal (inward) and centrifugal (outward) forces as they rotate in their orbits. Any such object that does not keep that balance falls to the center of its orbit or flies out into space. A ball thrown into the air falls back to the earth for the same reason. Electricity is the movement of electrons caused by the need of My Nature to balance the forces between positive and negative poles. It produces lightning, and it powers any electrical or electronic device.

For an airplane or a rocket to fly, a boat to float, or a wagon to roll, there is a constant interplay of opposing forces. They are there when an atom explodes, a volcano erupts, or a chemical reaction occurs. A gasoline engine uses many forms of them at once; so does a single living cell or a human being. As you breathe, walk, or run and as a plant lives and grows, these forces are ever present. Reflect again upon the delicate balance in nature—weather, climate, and ecology. In your own thinking, as you observe life around you, you will realize these are but a few examples of how these two Forces of My

Light, Positive and Negative Polarity, can be found in everything that exists. Look broadly, deeply, and carefully; you will see that they are there.

During the many lifetimes that you and all mankind have lived, sometimes you have obeyed My Spiritual Laws. At other times you did not. All of these experiences have been built into your soul, many of them with deep thought and feeling. Whenever you misused My Laws, you unbalanced My Polarity in your life, either too much to the Positive Pole or too much to the Negative One. Any unbalance of My Polarity curtails the flow of My Light into your life; and its stream is reduced in exact, direct proportion to the degree of unbalance. This is My Spiritual Law. When the current of My Light into your life is decreased, it brings to you a lack of My Life. This results in imperfect expression in whatever aspect of your life the unbalance occurs. You know this unbalance by many names. Disease, limitation, poverty, unhappiness, discord, and pain are but a few of them. All such defective or impaired conditions of the world are the direct result of negative response to My Light, disrupting the balance of the two Polarities. Realize, here, how even your very soul, as well as your physical, mental, and emotional well-being, is subject to My Law.

It is important for you to recognize, therefore, that you, and you alone, have created all of the negative conditions that exist in your life. You know that I have given you free will; and in your thinking, speaking, acting, and feeling in your present and all your past lifetimes, you have responded to the experiences your life has brought you completely of your own free will. Since I have given you free will, I always let you be absolutely free to do whatever you want to do in your life. You know I never interfere. Accordingly, by virtue of the fact that it is only you who have misused My Spiritual Law in your life, you can understand that you are solely responsible for that unbalance. And as you have free will, My Law does not correct any unbalance you have caused unless you freely allow My Law to work through you to do so by accepting My Will as your own. Hence, you are the only one who *can* enable Me to balance it; and if you will carefully consider what I Am explaining to you here, you cannot but agree that this is exactly as it should be.

For you to aspire toward Spiritual Mastery means that *you* are to seek Mastery of yourself and the material world. Someone else cannot do it for you—only you. This is what Spiritual Mastery is: For you to become the Master, *you must search for it and find it*. Of course, you know that you can attain it only in and through Me. Because I have given you free will, you are completely free to decide, of your own free will, whether or not and when you will let Me balance My Polarity in your life. You make this possible only when you learn My Spiritual Law and live within it. And this is true for all mankind.

Since it is My Nature to maintain a balanced Polarity and inasmuch as I Am the Spiritual Counterpart of your being, My Desire in you prompts you to desire to achieve that balance; it inspires you, eventually, to want to reach Mastery. This is the desire in human nature for a better, more moral, and more spiritual life, for goodness and, ultimately, spiritual perfection. It is an innate, human aspiration—the reason every culture has its religion and every religion is an exact expression of the spiritual consciousness of its followers. Still, to the extent that you do not respond to the Light of My Desire in you and heed its bidding, you dwell in the shadow of the unbalanced Polarity of negative action. Consequently, since all negative expression, when carried to full cycle, will eventually destroy itself, the negative of your unbalanced Polarity will, in its own time, bring to you its own degree of pain. To the degree that it does and to the extent that you do not respond to My Light, it eventually prods you to take the action necessary to restore the balance you have upset. So, no matter how you live your life, My Law teaches you to balance the Polarity of My Being—sooner or later. The Law of My Light pervades all of life entirely.

However, there is yet another feature of negative activity that it is important for you to understand. In direct proportion to your negative reaction to My Light in all your past experiences right up to this present moment, you have built negative habit-patterns into your soul. Religious scriptures often refer to a very negative soul as unclean as a result of evil deeds or sin. Of course, you realize that evil or sin is the misuse of My Law. It is negative—unbalanced—expression of My Spirit in you. These patterns are established in your soul as feelings or desires, some of them very deep. This is the reason some believe that destructive tendencies and desires for the lower life are innate in human nature, but this is not true. It could not be so since all of life comes forth from My Light. Those you find in your soul are merely your *own* creations that you have put there by means of negative living, and so it is for everyone.

Until you reach Mastery, then, you find two desires in your soul: one, to be positive or good; the other, to be negative or evil. It is the conflict between these two desires in you that you feel in the endeavors of your life. This struggle deeply pervades all humanity. Look at your history and at your world about you. From the Positive Desire comes My Still, Small Voice of Light; from the negative desire, the voice of darkness. As you live your life and as your soul gains experiences, it grows; and both forces in you, the positive and the negative, grow with you, each according to how much you permit your soul to give it expression in your everyday living.

To balance your Polarity, as your soul grows older and becomes wiser, there must come times in your life when you, of your own free will, decide to respond more to the positive expression of My Light rather than the negative. To adhere to the negative simply delays the fulfillment of your Destiny and results in more suffering for your soul. When you turn your mind to the positive, your desire for the spiritual Life of My Light increases in your consciousness. Your attention there intensifies it. Gradually, this desire, which is My Desire in you that you have accepted as your own, draws to you increasing amounts of My Light. As it enlightens your consciousness, it reveals to you a greater awareness of My Presence. So, when you decide of your own free will to continue more consistently to respond positively to that Desire and that Presence and turn away from the negative desires of your soul, ever-higher frequencies of My Light fill your consciousness, erasing its shadows and darkness.

You, the prodigal son, begin to return home to your Father's House of Love and Light. You hear and heed My Still, Small Voice, and I Am able to lead you, step by step, along the Path of My Light, enabling you to bring My Polarities to an ever-greater balance in your life until finally that balance is fully achieved. When this accomplishment is completely established in your soul and you have entirely entered into My Light, you will have reached your Destiny of Spiritual Mastery, you will have perfectly balanced the Positive and Negative Polarities of My Being in you and in your life, and you will have lifted your soul out of the negative expression of the world into the positive action of My Love. I, through you, will have re-established the balance of the Polarities of My Light in you forever. You will be a Master of My Light, a perfect Instrument for My Use. We will be One in consciousness, and you will ascend in Me into the Higher Realms of My Light for I will have raised you up *into* My Spirit *by* My Spirit. My Spiritual Law in you will be fulfilled.

CHAPTER XIV

My Love

My Light is My Love; and My Love is My Intelligence, My Energy, and My Substance. All activity, all movement, all occurrence is an expression of My Love. Even when it is negative, it is the power of My Love misused. My Love continuously draws to Me all things. Yet it gives Being, Life, Existence to all My Creations everywhere as it flows out to them and through them, forever returning in full cycle to Me, in time, to return again to them in an ever-finer frequency of My Light. It is always creative, constructive, inspiring, and beneficent. Since I Am all there is, there is no place My Love is not; and in it is contained all virtues, all fulfillment, and all completion.

My Love is the current of Life and is in constant flow. It is the essence of My Changelessness; still, it is the motivation of My Change—of My Unfoldment, ever upward toward My Perfection. The constancy of its Nature perpetually ushers forth into untold variations of My Expressions. My Love is My Desire for an ever-increasing awareness in consciousness of all attributes of My Being—of all My Creations. It is the Force that maintains the order of the universe, from the regularity of the stars in the heavens and the planets in their orbits to the integrity of the atom and the stability of the molecule. My Love is gravity, chemical change, electricity, and atomic power in action. Yes, every form of My Energy is an expression of My Love.

My Love is the sprouting of the seed, the growing of the plant, the budding of the flower, and the bearing of the fertilized fruit. It is the motivation of the mating call, of the copulation, and of the birth of all forms of life. It is the feeling of a mother for her offspring, of members of a family for one another, of a boy and girl in romantic attraction, of people in friendship, and of good-will of anyone toward all of life or any part of it. Even in death My Love is witnessed in many forms, as when someone gives his life to defend another person, a cause, or his country. Inasmuch as it is My Love that impels a soul into birth, so also does it draw him beyond the veil of material form when he relinquishes his earthly sojourn until another time.

From the foregoing, it is clear that the forms and expressions of My Love are as varied as My Expressions of Life themselves, as you find them in the world; therein is an infinite array of its kinds and degrees. They range from those of the densest physical substance to the human being and on to life so far advanced that it is beyond the conception of your mortal mind.

In My Love are all the attributes of My Light, and in My Light is the energy of your life. Hence, all of My Desires in you, which are various expressions of My Energy, are My Love that is ever leading, lifting, and inspiring you into a deeper and higher awareness of My Presence in you, in your life, and in the world. When you recognize My Desires in yourself and accept them as your own, you are responding to My Light and listening to My Voice. As you nourish those Desires, which are radiations of My Love, they cause your soul to grow and develop stronger and deeper into the qualities of My Being. These include all the virtues and all the noble qualities of character and personality that you attribute to Godliness and spirituality.

Remember, My Love is *the* food for your soul; and when you partake of it, you take on the attributes of that Love. Simply by feeding your life with My Love, your soul absorbs that nourishment; and that Love *becomes* the life, the substance, the expression, and the awareness of your soul. Just as your physical body assimilates what you eat, when you respond to My Love, you consume it into your soul.

It is My Life and My Energy coursing through you that gives you life. You recognize this Energy *as your life*—your thoughts, your actions, your feelings, and your desires. It inspires your wishes, your wants, and your motivations in your everyday living. Since all of your life is My Life flowing through you in physical, mental, emotional, and spiritual expression and because My Life is My Light and My Light is My Love, you can easily understand that your desires and feelings in conjunction with your thoughts and actions are manifestations of My Love in and through you. To be more exact, they *are* My Love in expression through you.

While there are many varied degrees and qualities of My Love, your soul becomes the excellence of spirituality in the proportion to which you make positive response to My Love. This virtuousness is determined by the extent to which you balance My Polarities in your life and by the height of the vibrations of My Light that you attain. My Love is the innate tendency of My Nature to balance My Polarities as My Life unfolds through you into ever-greater expressions of consciousness. This tendency is My Desire to ever maintain the balance of My Polarities.

Since you are My Creation, made in My Image, you inherit all the attributes of My Nature. So it is also your nature to desire to balance them in your life.

To whatever extent you aspire to the higher Spiritual Life, you are responding to My Desire in you. Whenever you do not, you are giving life to the desires of the unbalanced Polarity of your soul. Still, you are using the Energy of My Life, My Love, when you give expression to these negative desires. As I have said before, I let you be free to do that so you can bring to yourself the experiences you need to enable you to learn that My Will is your will—that your fulfillment in life can be realized only when you do My Will, only when you live completely in My Love and within My Spiritual Law.

Now, from all that I have told you here, you can realize that every occurrence in the universe is an expression of My Love, My Desire, working through My Creations, inspiring and unfolding them into an ever-higher consciousness of My Being, which is a constantly greater spiritual awareness in themselves, from the atom to the human and beyond. So it is only natural that this is also the same with you.

Therefore, your desire for the Higher Life is My Desire in you to lead you into Oneness in consciousness with Me in order to enable Me to balance My Polarity in your life. Your desire for that Union is your love for Me, for the Spiritual Life. Understanding, then, that it is My Love that ever so gently, caressingly, and gradually draws, leads, inspires, and lifts you into Oneness in consciousness with Me, it becomes your responsibility to nourish the flame of your desire, your love, for the greater conscious and subconscious awareness of My Presence in you, in your life, and in your world until it burns fiercely and powerfully for the Higher Life. It is this Desire, this Love, that sets the forces in motion for your spiritual unfoldment and your ultimate Union with Me as it awakens you to seek the greater Light of My Being.

So, if you are truly seeking Spiritual Mastery, it is essential that you take every opportunity that Life brings you to live in the balanced Polarity of My Love at all times. Yet, remember, the growth of your spiritual consciousness is a very gradual process as it develops in perfect harmony with My Law. Still, the progress you make is determined by how conscientiously and determinedly you pursue it. Consequently, since you do not achieve the consciousness of My Divine Love all at once, you must cultivate in your thinking, speaking, acting, and feeling the highest frequencies of My Love of which your soul is capable at the moment, ever aspiring to rise to yet finer degrees of it until you finally reach My Divine, Impersonal Love and establish it into your consciousness. Use your Silence and your Meditations to lift yourself into the conscious awareness of these higher vibrations and, then, to utilize this greater love to nourish your body, mind, and soul so it can carry you continuously upward on the Path of My Light.

When your love for the Higher Life becomes a burning spiritual flame, it also serves another important function as you travel the Path of My Light. Your love for Me becomes a consuming desire in your heart and mind; and your soul is filled to overflowing with a great radiance of the Light of My Love, forming a beautiful, powerful sphere of My Light completely interpenetrating and surrounding you. As a result, you dwell in My Light, and it abides in you and all around you.

Any negative patterns, desires, or tendencies you may have established in your soul in this or in any of your past incarnations are no real temptation in the presence of your yet more potent love for Oneness with Me—your mighty desire for your realization in consciousness of the positive, balanced expression of the Polarities of My Light. It enables you to stand firm and strong in My Light, even though some of those negative patterns may be titanic forces in your consciousness as you are learning to correct and harmonize them.

Such a desire anchors you deeply in My Light and to My Inner Guidance. With it, you are able to draw upon the entire resources of My Love—the unlimited strength and power of God. It becomes a complete protection and security for you as you walk the Path of My Light. Thus, you are able to abide solely in My Peace. All of this is because you live in My Light as you respond to My Love; and in My Spiritual Light, no force of darkness can reach you. So, no negative condition can enter your life. *You are protected by My Light.*

Accordingly, it is very important for you to remember always that in traveling the Path of My Light to Spiritual Mastery, My Love is your *only* protection. This, then, is another vital reason for the necessity of fanning the fire of your love for Me, increasing your desire to come into My Presence in consciousness until it is a consuming spiritual flame in your soul. This is why it is of paramount importance for everyone who aspires for Spiritual Mastery to rely eventually *only* upon My Light and all of its attributes for their guidance and protection in meeting and overcoming all negative conditions, circumstances, situations, and things My Law brings to them as they journey along Life's Way. Hence, you realize, of course, that this is also true for you.

In your everyday living in the physical plane, then, though it is necessary for you to place your faith and trust in people and in conditions of the material world, underlying it all, your ultimate faith must be in Spirit—the spiritual expression of My Light, which is the true Reality—and not in the unreal appearance of negative worldly circumstances. Your deeper faith must be in Me, in My Spirit that eternally dwells within you and within all those who enter your life as well as those who do not, whoever or wherever they may be on earth. You know I have told you that you shall have no other gods before Me, and you understand that it is necessary for you to live within My Law in order to reside in My Light, in My Peace, in My Protection, and in My Love.

CHAPTER XV

Degrees of My Love

Now, dear seeker of the Inner Mysteries, you have a portrayal of the countless manifestations of My Love that abound in the world that you know. In addition to these, however, as you look at Life again, another view will reveal itself to you. In your life and in the lives of the entire human race, there are three major degrees of My Love about which you should know. They are: physical love, soul love, and Divine or Impersonal Love. Yet, as I describe them to you, considering each one separately, understand that there is no clear division or demarcation among them as you give expression to these phases of My Love in your everyday living. Each blends into the other, and they intermingle in an infinite variety of ways. In every soul there are elements of each at all times expressing in its own degree according to his spiritual consciousness and the positive or negative response to life that he makes each moment of time.

97

The lowest form of human love is physical love. Although it is a lower vibration than soul love or Impersonal Love, in its pure form it is a very wonderful and positive expression of My Life. It is a necessary, fundamental love of all animate life, including the human, that ensures the propagation of all species of My Creation. It inspires the physical attraction of one human being for another. Numerous friendships are initiated by this love, and many men and women are drawn together in marriage by it. It is a personal, possessive love, a love for the fulfillment and satisfaction of personal desires. One who has this love directs it to those who help to satisfy his own individual needs and wants.

In the mind and life of man, however, it has too often become debased, carrying him, sometimes, lower in vibration than the animals below him in evolution. In this negative condition, he finds himself bound by the habit-patterns of lust, wasting his Life Force until, often too late, he finally realizes the price he must pay to lift it again to its original purity. In his evolution, mankind has come into the awareness of good and evil; and of his own free will, he must learn to choose to balance the Polarity of My Light in his life. A very great lesson he has to learn in order to attain Spiritual Mastery is to lift his sex-force, one of the avenues of expression of his total Life Force, into positive response to My Love. He

Fun·da·mental

will achieve this when he learns to generate, regenerate, and, finally, fully transmute his sex-force into the Divine, Impersonal Love of My Being, which will be another one of his accomplishments when he unites in consciousness with Me.

As those who are drawn together by physical love live their lives among themselves, their physical love usually grows deeper into a higher form of love. It becomes rooted in their souls, and so it is often called soul love. As you experience it in your life, it is the love of your soul for another soul. Such a love *Soul* is not inspired so much by physical appearance or other physical attributes; instead, it is induced by the beautiful qualities of the soul. Thus, it includes physical love, but it goes beyond that, penetrating into your soul and creating a lasting bond therein. Although it is still a personal, possessive love, it is stronger, broader, and more profound.

Usually there is a greater amount of harmony, understanding, and identity among people who have attained a soul love for one another. Remembering that this love is an expression of My Love in human consciousness, it, too, draws together people in friendships and man and woman in marriage when it has already been developed between them in some previous incarnation or, possibly, earlier in the present one. Friendships, marriage, and all human relationships built upon this kind of love are more permanent and stable than those founded solely upon physical love since the source of attraction is in the heartfelt emotions of the soul. In a much wider view, it is soul love that has drawn you into your family, community, nation, race, religion, etc.

As your love continues to develop, becoming purer, deeper, and stronger, you gradually begin to realize a yet higher form of My Love. It is Spiritual Love—My Divine, Impersonal Love. Whereas purely physical love is a love that is mainly selfish for personal self-gratification and self-fulfillment of individual needs and wants, and whereas soul love is dominantly a possessive love that is concerned for the happiness and welfare of those you love, Spiritual Love is the Love for all of Life that emanates equally to every part of it. It always includes the two lower forms of love, but it lifts your soul above and beyond their essence into a yet more noble expression of consciousness. It redeems and transmutes the love of your lower nature into Spirit. When you raise your awareness into the higher frequencies of Impersonal Love, you give your love to all of Life as the sun shines its light, radiating to everything that comes into your presence without thought or concern of return. You cease to think of self; instead, your thoughts dwell only on the objects of your love. Since you love all of Life, your desires and motivations are solely to devote yourself to its service—to help your fellowman and all of My Creations that come into your life.

Even in your present consciousness, there are times when you experience My Divine Love; but to lift yourself into Spiritual Mastery requires that you train your soul to live only in this Love at all times. It must be nourished to be developed; you cannot will it to be in a moment—it comes with time. Neither can you truly know its essence until you fully experience it. To achieve it, deeply desire it; and grasp the highest concept of love that you know, and live in it. As you aspire to respond to My Impersonal Love in your Silence, Meditations, and everyday living, I will gradually draw you into the full awareness of its universal consciousness.

This Divine Love can be realized by you only to the extent that you, in positive response to My Light, balance the Polarities of My Spiritual Law. Therefore, any negative conditions that you may find in your soul must be harmonized and redeemed into the finer, positive vibrations of Spirit. Patterns of unbalanced sex expression must be corrected. Replace fear with faith and courage, hate with love and forgiveness. Purge your soul of all the dross of your consciousness. Rectify your thinking, speaking, acting, and feeling so that you permit only the pure impressions of Spirit to enter your soul. There is nothing to prevent you from achieving it if you are willing to pay the price in self-discipline, application, dedication, and faith.

You know that to whatever degree you have learned to hate, you are living on the negative side of My Law. Yet the Law of My Love does not change even when it is unbalanced. It brings you together with the persons or conditions that are the objects of your hate until you learn to bring the harmony of My Love into your life as you meet yourself in them in your everyday living; to live with them in the positive action of My Love.

This is why you draw interpersonal relationships and conditions into your life with which you have conflict, tension, strife, hatred, fear, and other negative feelings or circumstances. They occur in your experiences in exactly the same proportion that you have those identical negative qualities in your own soul, which you have placed there sometime in the past, and to the degree that My Law is bringing those vibrations to you now for correction. It is the reason many people in marital, personal, and business relationships find their own varying amounts of unfulfilled dreams of what their life should be. In differing depths, they have established into their souls feelings of hurt, bitterness, dislike, and other negative impressions and have inflicted the same upon others. Thus, their own souls are drawing to them the equivalent measure of what they have given in the past; and they are required to work through these relationships until they can respond to them only in My Love in order to correct the negative patterns in their souls and balance the Polarity of My Light in their consciousness.

Compassion is a quality of My Impersonal Love, and it is natural for you to have feeling for those who are meeting in themselves some of the pains of life. You feel for them because your soul has suffered as they do. That is complete understanding; that *is* My Love. You fully comprehend what they are experiencing. Yet, it is very important for you to realize that, as a traveler on the Path of My Light, you must not enter into the negative feelings with them. As you rise above any negative condition, it becomes your responsibility never to permit yourself to indulge in those negative thoughts or feelings again.

An easy way for you to remember this aspect of My Love is to make a distinction between the words *compassion* and *sympathy*. Since compassion is an attribute of My Love, when you feel it, that is what you feel—My Love. Hence, you do not feel the negativity of suffering in any of its degrees or forms although you do have the full cognition of it—a vivid awareness of the memories of past experiences. Your resultant feeling, then, is an understanding Love *for* the one who is suffering. This is the Christ compassion. On the other hand, sympathy is usually defined as feeling *with* or entering into the same emotions as one who is experiencing negative expression. Since they are negative, when you partake of their feelings, at that moment, you become negative.

Therefore, although you clearly comprehend the distress of others and would do anything to help to relieve their condition in a positive way, still, you cannot permit your mind and emotions to come down in vibration to theirs and enter into the negativity of their lives. If you do, you again descend into the same unbalanced condition of My Polarity out of which you have risen, or may be rising, in consciousness. In allowing it, you would be in a negative or weakened condition similar to theirs while extending any assistance to them—the weak aiding the weak or the blind leading the blind. When your life is at its peak in positive expression, when you are living only in My Love, you have much greater spiritual strength and wisdom with which to render assistance. So, as you advance spiritually, it becomes more important for you to learn not to feel *with* negative situations, but to feel *for* them.

It is in My Impersonal Love that you find the Oneness of all of Life. In this higher frequency of My Love, you experience the greater power and depth of My Being. Therefore, your feeling for all of Life is also more profound. Your Love is deeper and stronger. Yet, you do not hold any object of your affections in any possessive way. You are aware that it is a segment of My Life in expression and that it is all a portion of My Being. To the extent that you recognize that you *are* Me, you know that all of Life is an integral part of you. Since we are One, you inherit My Kingdom. Possession has no meaning in this awareness. In the Oneness of My Love, you are a part of the whole; and as a part, you partake of the whole. You live in the universal consciousness of My Omnipresence.

As you lift yourself into the finer vibrations of My Love, you are able to free yourself of any need to grasp anything possessively for yourself alone. In consciousness, you release it, as the nature of My Love is only to give, not to take in any personal way. You transmute the self of your personal, human existence into the selflessness of My Spiritual Being. Your love, taking on the qualities of My Love, radiates bountifully and uniformly to all of life. And as it does, it draws to you an ever greater quantity of its abundance from My Divine Supply.

All that receive your love return love to you; according to their capability, they send back their own, each in proportion to its consciousness of My Love. When you take objects of your love into your heart, you hold them tenderly and gently as only My Love enables you to do; but as you live in My Light, you are able to release them freely in consciousness at any moment and for any amount of time that My Law may call upon you to let them go. But always remember, My Love is always steadfast, faithful, loyal, and true.

Listen closely to My Guidance as I, your Still, Small Voice, speak to you from the inner recesses of your Being, and I will reveal to you where you stand on the Path of My Light in your spiritual awareness of My Love. Then, as you live within My Spiritual Law, I, through you, will gradually and steadily build into your life the ever-higher frequencies of My Love until it blossoms forth into the supreme, radiant brilliance of My Divine, Impersonal Love.

CHAPTER XVI

Faith

Now, you know that Spirit is the true Reality—the real essence of My Being—and that all material expression and form are simply manifestations of lower vibrations of My Spiritual Light. You also understand that the current of My Light and My Love is constantly flowing in and through the physical plane, giving everything therein its existence and consciousness. Moreover, you realize that you are a part of that evolution and that, as a member of the human kingdom, it is your Destiny, one day, to enable Me to transmute your physical Temple and your soul, in your Ascension, into the spiritual consciousness of My Light. And in addition to all of this, you are aware that in the planes of My Life above the physical, there are uncounted worlds within worlds that extend into the infinity of My Being.

In your gradual, upward spiral toward Spiritual Mastery, you must progress through your human consciousness. Therefore, since you are living more on the Negative Polarity of My Light, your awareness is centered to a greater extent in the material plane, in your physical body and its senses, and in your conscious mind. As you know, your conscious mind is a finite mind; and inasmuch as you depend mostly upon your fleshly senses for the knowledge about My Life that your mind uses in your everyday living, its awareness is chiefly restricted to the material world.

Furthermore, because you have unbalanced My Polarities in your world, your mind, through your senses, is able to perceive life as you know it mainly in its unbalanced state. And the physical faculties of your body and mind limit the dimensions of your world; for most, they permit only a very vague awareness of the actuality of the far vaster realms of My Spirit. The reality that you perceive, then, is not only restricted substantially to empirical knowledge, but, since My Polarity is unbalanced on this earth, the reality of My Life that you do know is even distorted. This is the reason why religions so universally have taught that this world and the things of it are illusion, maya, mere appearance, and foolishness, as seen in the eyes of God.

Accordingly, mankind for the most part has accepted life to be what his physical senses have told him. This material view of My Life has become deeply embedded into his culture as it has developed throughout the ages. It has such a profound impact upon the minds of his children that they, too, believe what it teaches them. So, this narrow and false conception of My Reality is also perpetuated by the negative thought-force of humanity. As it is generally perceived, then, the human consciousness recognizes it as fact—unquestioned empirical fact—while the reality of spirit is relegated to the status of mere belief. All that is experienced by man's physical senses is seen as the reality of My Life as it is in the world. Since it is dominantly the only world he knows, it is primarily the *only reality he knows*—it *is* reality to him. Even highly evolved spiritual souls struggle to lift this veil.

Looking at Life from the expanded, spiritual perspective, this material outlook of the human race falls into the same class as the beliefs that the world is flat and that the sun rotates around the earth, as was believed a few centuries ago. Similarly, the world accepts negative conditions also as part of the reality of its life. Disease, fear, hate, lack, limitation, poverty, starvation, death, aging, and all other imperfections of life are acknowledged as elements of this apparent realness too. As a result, mankind concludes that such conditions have power over him, over his life, and over the lives of others generally.

Thus, man's human faith is placed in the unreality of the negative, material world. Since he does not want a negative condition to affect him, too often he fears it as he looks for ways to avoid it. You know that fear is faith in negative expression, the lack of faith in Spirit. In feeling fear of something, you are having faith that a negative condition can affect you. You believe that it can do so; and as long as you believe that, it can. Fear being the opposite or negative expression of faith, resulting from the misuse of My Spiritual Law, My Law brings to you the product of your own creation: *You bring the object of your fear upon yourself*.

So it is with all negative conditions of the world. They enter your life because you hold your faith in them. When you believe in them—in their ability to influence your life—that is where your faith is fixed, not in the reality of My Light and the positive expression of My Law. Hence, they do have power over you as long as you believe they can affect you. It is *always* because you *believe* in them. Your world takes on the patterns of your mind as you build them into the feelings of your soul in your everyday thinking, feeling, speaking, and acting. This is where the faith of the masses of the world resides today: in the imperfect, limited, negative consciousness of materiality. They do not believe in My Spiritual Law. *Most do not even know it exists, nor do they know Me*.

Does it seem at all possible for you to realize that the moment you cease to have faith in the negative conditions of the unbalanced Polarity of My Light, they can no longer enter your life? *None* of them can reach you, not disease, fear, lack, limitation, failure, aging, or any other—not even death! Of course, this means that you place your faith in Me and in the spiritual reality of My Balanced Polarity. Since I Am Perfection, when you place your faith in My Perfection and in My Spiritual Law and establish that faith in your consciousness, mentally and emotionally, then you attract to yourself that perfection and the fulfillment of all objects of your faith.

Law of Att.

In your spiritual unfoldment, as you draw closer in consciousness to Me and to My Light, the veil is gradually lifted; and you are able to realize an increasingly greater sensitivity to the reality of My Spirit. As My Spiritual Reality becomes more vivid in your awareness, you are able to recognize, in this greater Light, that the reality of the material world as you have known it is far different and far less significant than what it has seemed to you before. In addition, you can more clearly perceive the gross distortion of that which is there in negative expression.

As you balance the Positive and Negative Polarities of My Light, the dominance of the negative, material world decreases, receding to its proper place and permitting the Positive Polarity of My Light to regain its rightful prominence and influence in your life. As this happens, you experience a growing awareness of My Presence within you until you finally become as conscious of My Spiritual Reality as you presently are of your physical reality. When this is achieved in your consciousness, then you will know that you and I are One. Your faith in Me and in My Spiritual Law will be as great as it currently is in the physical laws of the material plane in which you live. Moreover, it will be infinitely more deeply anchored in My Love than it now is in the unreality of the negative expression of your world. You will be able to see My Life in the full expression of My Light and realize the true nature and essence of My Being. Nevermore will fear enter your life because it will no longer hold your faith. Its tenacious grip will be broken forever.

It is important for Me to clarify here a common misconception about fear. It is often seen as a needed, natural, constructive emotion, a safeguard that people should use to protect themselves against danger of any kind. Hence, it is believed that if something harmful is feared, it will be avoided. Of course, it is universally recognized that it is a natural, normal human reaction for anyone to evade any threatening situation or condition if he cannot otherwise control the danger it poses. This is even true of many forms of My Life below the human in consciousness. It is an instinctive reaction of life for its own protection and survival. Also, it is certain that if you remove yourself from danger because you are afraid of it, at that moment of getting away from it, it cannot affect you.

However, it is very important for the student of Spiritual Mastery to understand that *any fear of any kind and of any degree of intensity is negative*—an expression of the unbalanced Polarity of My Light. In My Light, fear does not exist. It abides only in the lives of those who misuse My Spiritual Law. When you fear, you *feel* that fear; and in so feeling, you build it into your soul in the exact proportion as the depth of the emotion and the length of time you permit yourself to indulge in it. As a consequence, you not only experience it at the moment, but you also set the forces in motion that, in due time, will bring conditions into your life that will cause you to come face to face with that very fear, again and again, until you finally respond to My Light and remove it from your soul. All of this is My Spiritual Law. Learn it well and obey it.

Those who believe fear to be a means of protection do not understand My Spiritual Law nor do they fully realize the implications of fear. When anyone is burned by something hot, he learns to avoid any hot object that would burn him. In the same way, he learns to move away from any danger that threatens him if he cannot control it. Fears develop as a result of frightening experiences or cultural conditioning. A child may be frightened by an animal or his parents may teach him to fear it. Therefore, it seems natural and normal for anyone to fear. It is certainly human, but *all fears* are *learned*; in My Light, they are not natural nor innate, not one of them. Any fear in your soul that is not learned in this lifetime was created by you in a previous incarnation.

Moreover, to avoid a danger does not mean that you must fear it. You know, yourself, that you evade many hazards without feeling fear. Fear is a negative *feeling*, although it does always have its accompanying thought. You know boiling water will harm you, and you have learned to elude its dangers; yet, you can be closely associated with it every day, knowing the risk you take, but not have any *feeling* of fear. Your mind only discerns and comprehends. From experience, you have come to understand and to respect the properties of heat. Hence, ordinarily, everyone keeps away from such perils, not out of fear, but as a result of understanding and respect. In the same way, you can perceive any negative condition with your mind, recognize its dangers, and take any action necessry to protect yourself; but you do not in any way need to experience fear to do it, either in your mind or in your emotions. However, since you have conditioned yourself to fear, as has this entire human race, to entirely remove it from your life, it is necessary for you to retrain yourself not to fear.

It is universally recognized that any frightening experience can incite fear. Such incidents can be averted by controlling them or by escaping from them. But, any fear you may feel in no way helps you to avoid the danger. In fact, it only interferes. It can immobilize you if it is strong enough; it can even cause your death. Stagefright, momentary mental and physical helplessness, and heart attacks are not uncommon occurences resulting from fright the world over.

When you are confronted with any fearful encounter in life, if you keep your mind, body, and emotions quiet and controlled, they are in a much more efficient condition to more effectively cope with it. You are able to think more clearly and decisively, and you can respond more positively, both physically and emotionally, to the negative condition. If not before, it should be obvious to you by now that fear of any kind or degree can never improve your chances of safety. It can only make them worse.

Your fears are your faith in the negative conditions of the world of appearance. They are your lack of faith in My Spiritual Law and in My Spiritual Reality. They are the result of your acceptance of and belief in the unbalanced Polarity of My Light— the negative conditions of your mundane life. Since you are responsible for that unbalance in your life, when you permit yourself to indulge in fears, they become your creations, and yours alone. Inasmuch as you, too, are a creator, your creations, even though negative, still follow the action of My Law. They draw to you their own fulfillment. To indulge in fears, then, is to bring the result of those fears, in time, into your life. By fearing, you cause My Law to materialize the very conditions of which you are afraid; and you perpetually draw the fear and the feared condition into your life until you eliminate it from your subconscious mind.

Since you realize that fear can cause only negative conditions in your life and that it can never protect you, you can understand why it is necessary for you to learn never to permit yourself to indulge in it. How do you do this? When you keep your attention centered with Me and when you consistently live in My Light, you put your full faith in My Spiritual Law and My Divine Protection. As you live in My Light, you know that darkness cannot enter therein. Darkness cannot exist in Light. In view of the fact that fear is negative and because anything that is negative is of the realm of darkness, neither can it enter your life when you reside in My Light. And any fears already established in the consciousness of your soul become gradually weaker until they finally disappear because you no longer give them life for their existence. This happens because you discontinue to hold your faith in your fears and cease to direct the energy of My Life, as it courses through your Temple, into such negative channels of mental and emotional expression.

As you live in perfect faith in My Light, then, it guides you and protects you in every instance from any danger. In this response to My Light, when this faith is fully consummated in your consciousness, to avoid or even to have a need to protect yourself from fear has no meaning in your life. You simply live constantly in My Spiritual Light, and it invariably protects you. Of course, to be able to receive the complete protection of My Light requires that you live entirely in My Light; and this occurs only after considerable progress has been achieved in spiritual development and unfoldment. To attain it, it is necessary to enter the training for Spiritual Mastery.

In traveling the Path of My Light, it is vitally important for you to recognize any negative condition or circumstance that you may meet along the way and to use every positive means you know to protect yourself. But it is equally essential that you keep your attention centered with Me and in My Light and not permit it to be taken into the negative vibrations confronting you. By doing this, you are able to "see only with your eyes," which means you perceive them solely with your mind; but you do not accept them, you do not permit your mind nor your emotions to enter into those negative vibrations,

thus preventing them from reaching your soul.
When your attention is centered with Me, you live
only in perfect faith in the protection of My Light.

As you walk along Life's Way in My Light, to the
greatest extent that you can realize the truth of what
I have told you here, place your faith in the reality
of My Spirit and My Spiritual Law. Cease to hold
your faith in any negative conditions of the world
that only bind you to the consciousness and expression of those conditions—lack, limitation, imperfec-
tion, fear, hate, and all such unbalanced vibrations.
They are there only because you believe in them.
Their reality exists to you simply because you put
your faith in them—the only reason they can and do
affect you. By accepting them as real, you incor-
porate them into the patterns of your soul.

The moment you remove negative impressions
from your consciousness, they no longer remain in
your life. They are not of My Light nor of your
heritage in My Kingdom. Listen to Me as I quietly
speak to you from the inner recesses of your Being,
and follow carefully My Guidance you receive. Your
faith in Me will set you free—completely free—as
your awareness of the spiritual reality of My Presence within you comes into the foreground of your
consciousness, revealing to you the true essence of
My Being in the intensely vivid experience of the
balanced Polarity of My Light that it manifests
to you.

CHAPTER XVII

Your Faith in My Truth

Almost everyone has some idea of the meaning of faith, but a yet deeper understanding of it would help most of them, if not all, to attain a greater awareness of the inner Life of My Light. Let Me speak to you about it now in more general terms. Faith can be defined as an awareness of and belief in My Spiritual Truth which cannot be *proven* or shown to exist by means of the things of the outer, material world. You have been taught that it is the substance of things hoped for and the evidence of things not seen. It is because of the vast diversity in the consciousness of human beings that the mortal mind has such a great leeway for interpretation of the *things* not seen. And this is the reason for the huge variety of beliefs in the world today.

My Inner Spiritual World is the real World. The material world is a passing, changing, unreal world. Your physical senses are the means by which you have an awareness of and contact with this outer, physical plane; but you also have an inner sense by which you can reach the true World of My Spirit. However, your physical senses bring to you such a vivid impression of the material world that you tend to recognize it as reality. It occupies the attention of most people to the point of dominating their thinking and even their entire consciousness.

Yet, there always remains with everyone a certain cognition of his inner sense of the reality of My Being. This inward Knowing is stronger in some and weaker in others according to their spiritual consciousness. It cannot be verified in the outer, material world, weighed or experimented with in the laboratory, or proven by the empirical, scientific method. It is not even felt by the physical senses. However, it is this intrinsic, inmost discernment of My Presence that causes mankind to believe in Me and in My Inner Spiritual Reality, each perceiving it in proportion to his own spiritual consciousness. This belief he calls faith. It cannot be given by one person to another for it is born of a personal experience between God and each individual soul— between Me and you, alone.

One with great faith, though, can *inspire* faith in others by leading them into a greater awareness of My Presence. This occurs when they react positively to My Light in the one whose faith is strong; and in responding to Me in him, they experience a deeper consciousness of Me in themselves. This lifts them into a higher spiritual realization of the reality of My Presence, causing their faith in My Spirit to grow stronger.

As it is for all mankind, it is your Divine Destiny to direct your attention to your own inherent consciousness of My Spirit within you until you completely recognize the truth of My Reality and allow Me to direct you in all of your affairs. In doing this, you are able to see the outer, material world in its true light and realize its essence as it is seen through My Eyes. When you know My Reality in this way, you can then conduct your life by the correct perception of My Being and the unerring guidance of My Still, Small Voice. Thus, your life will always be lived in a constructive way for yourself and for all others who enter it, and you will know the peace of My Light.

In the world in which you live, it is the result of this emphasis upon the physical plane of life that causes so many to get a distorted concept of the reality of My Truth. This is especially accentuated by the development and widespread use of the experimental, scientific method which seeks empirical knowledge and tends to cause mankind to look for *proof* for any truth *before* he will accept it as such. And this is not meant as a denouncement of the scientific method in any way. It is a wonderful discovery of man, and it has its proper place in his search for empirical truth. Moreover, when it is correctly understood and applied, it can be just as effective in his quest for My Spiritual Truth.

Yet in God is contained all Knowledge, all Wisdom, and all Truth. In Him, I Am all there is to know and to be. As I have told you, there is no purpose for Me to verify Myself to mankind; it is his responsibility to come to the realization of My Presence within himself—to lead himself into the awareness of My Reality. In like manner, he must prove My Truth to himself. In this way, he can apply the scientific method in his search for My Spiritual Truth.

How do you do this? If you expect to observe your world in the physical plane and see therein the positive expression of My Truth, too frequently you will be greatly disappointed because the world does not always live according to My Light. Instead, it is necessary for you to use your Silence and Meditations to lift your vibrations so you can hear the Inner Voice of My Presence within you and learn My Truth as I reveal it to you. Then you must put it into application in your daily living in everything you do until it manifests in perfect expression in your life. When you do this, you demonstrate to yourself its reality. Hence, as you learn the truth of My Spiritual Law, you live within the Law, following it in faith, alone, until you have proven to yourself its validity; and you do this by living it first and then watching it come forth in expression in your material world.

Let Me briefly restate what I have said here. In using the empirical, scientific method, you prove the existence of a physical law by careful experimentation, and then you accept it as fact and put your faith in it. To prove to yourself the reality of My Spiritual Law, once I have brought it to your conscious awareness from within you, you first accept it as fact, put your full faith in it, and live within it; then My Truth substantiates your faith as My Law is fulfilled in your life. So there must be a readiness in your soul before your conscious mind can recognize and accept My Truth when I reveal it to you. Also, be constantly reminded that you can never expect anyone, not even Life itself, to prove My Truth to you; you, and you alone, must prove it to yourself.

Now, this does not mean that you cannot observe My Laws unfolding in the world. On the contrary, there are many instances where you can see them. But, there are also numerous occasions in which it can seem to anyone who does not have a full understanding of My Spiritual Truth that My Laws are not always valid. It can even appear that the opposite of My Laws is true. And these are the incidents that can cause the inexperienced seeker of My Truth to stumble and even lose faith in My Laws because, as he sees it in the world or in his own life, they do not work or, at best, they do not always work.

An example of this may be seen in My Spiritual Law of Cause and Effect. This Law states that as you sow so shall you reap. In other words, according to the way you live your life, so must you receive the consequences that it brings. Thus, if you give in kindness, you will receive in kindness; or if you do everything with love in your heart, you will always receive in love from others. However, there are many examples in the world in which people are kind and loving, but who have been grossly mistreated by their fellowman with unkindness and ill-feeling, sometimes even with cruelty and hatred. Many such instances abound. There are those who gain wealth dishonestly; yet, life often seems to continue to bless them with more. Some inflict great injury on others, but ostensibly go unscathed themselves. Others struggle with all their might to reach a goal; still, many of them do not reach it. Innocent people are sometimes punished for crimes they did not do.

These apparent exceptions to My Spiritual Law are so common in the world that the masses of humanity give little real credence to its validity. Their faith is too frequently broken by unfulfilling experiences. What little faith is left is usually scattered among the many facets of their material existence.

They reason that My Law, to be Law, must be consistently so; and the constancy they expect in it, they do not find. Too many grope their way, not really knowing where to put their faith. The reality of My Law has little meaning to them. While all of this is happening, I Am constantly endeavoring to awaken them to a realization of its genuine actuality, patiently waiting for centuries for their spiritual unfoldment so I can lead them into Union with Me in consciousness.

So the younger soul, emerging into My Greater Light, too often does not wholly comprehend how My Spiritual Law works out. Though it is always fulfilled, it invariably takes its own time in its fulfillment. As My Law is stated, past causes bring about effects that result in present experiences. Some of these causes could have occurred many lifetimes ago when this soul was not so experienced and wise and when it did not have as clear an awareness of good and evil, perhaps not even knowing there was such a thing as Spiritual Law. Of course, the causes could just as well have been more recent. It all depends upon their own time of fulfillment.

As you go along Life's Way, if you have no conscious memory of the causes of the current experiences that are affecting you, unless you realize the full implications of the operation of My Law, it would seem to you that it is bringing into your life some things for which you are not responsible—that you did not cause. But that it never does. Get it clear in your mind and deep in your memory that whatever may be the circumstances you find in your life, you are the one who put them there and no one else. When you entirely understand My Law, however, you can permanently anchor your faith in it, allowing it to grow so powerfully strong that you can veritably move mountains. In such faith as this, you rest peacefully in the infinite strength, stability, and protection of My Light. You become a powerful soul.

Remember, every experience has a spiritual lesson to teach you. If in positive response to My Law, however, you have already learned what any one of them is intended to impress upon you, it may have little to impart to you. Nevertheless, it is My Spiritual Law that you must harmonize all negative energy you have set in motion. When My Law returns that energy to you for you to redeem through experiences that it brings into your life, it gives you the chance to do just that. This is the way you pay your karmic debts. It is for this reason that the further you travel on the Path of My Light, the more you will recognize every negative obstacle to be but an opportunity to take another step in your progress toward Spiritual Mastery.

Moreover, because you are unable to perceive consciously the cause of any effect that my Law draws to you nor the effect of any cause you may presently initiate does not mean in any way that My Law is not fulfilled in its own time and in its own way, perhaps differently than your conscious mind may expect. God is not mocked, and My Spiritual Laws are eternally immutable; they are as constant as the laws of gravity and mathematics. Such Truths you must accept in faith as My Light reveals them to your conscious awareness until you attain sufficient illumination of My Light to enable you to know their reality.

It is important, therefore, to remember that if you sincerely desire to attain a higher place in your spiritual consciousness, it is essential that you learn My Spiritual Laws from My Guidance within you, believe in them, place your full faith in them, and constantly apply them in your everyday living until they become an integral part of your consciousness, no matter what the outer appearances of your life may seem to be and regardless of how long it may take you to do it. It is paramount that you live in the perfect faith of My Light until My Law is fulfilled in your life. This is the price you must pay in order to receive your inheritance in My Kingdom—the achievement in your life of the unlimited supply of My Abundance.

In summary, as you seek My Truth, it is necessary that you verify the reality of My Spiritual Laws for yourself; and you alone must do it. Yet, it is essential that you confirm them in and through Me. My Laws must be applied and lived in their positive expression *before* they will so manifest in your outer world, and it is vital that you embrace them of your own free-will choice. Your world, as it is, will not give you sufficient verification because it does not live completely in the balanced Polarity of My Being. Hence, as a student of My Light, it is your task to implant in yourself an ever-increasing faith in this deeper understanding of My Truth as you live it every day. Then, when My Spiritual Laws are fulfilled in your life, in your consciousness, you will realize perfect faith in them; and you will fully experience the complete awareness of the Truth of My Light.

CHAPTER XVIII

My Happiness

My dear aspirant for the higher Life, all the world is ever searching to find My Happiness, and few there are who find it. The reason for this is that the souls of most people are too deeply immersed in the negative Polarity of My Light—in the materiality of the physical plane. My Happiness does not exist in worldliness. It flourishes only in the perfect balance of the two Polarities of My Light, the Positive and the Negative. Yet there are many degrees of happiness, ranging from pure physical pleasure to the heavenly bliss of the Spiritual Realms. Happiness is more enduring and more constant as you come into the higher vibrations of My Being. Its degree increases in direct proportion to the increase of the frequencies of My Light. So the more you respond to My Light, the closer you come to Me in consciousness, the happier you will be— the higher quality and quantity of happiness you will experience.

129

Happiness is a state of mind or consciousness; it is your response to your own awareness of the fulfillment in your consciousness of a greater expression of My Light. All of the experiences of people in the world that induce happiness result from their own perception of that accomplishment. Even in negative activity, they are using its own measure of My Light, but in its unbalanced Polarity, when they enjoy its fascination and delight in their indulgence in it. In so doing, they do gain soul experience, but on the negative side of My Light Rays, which they will be required to balance some day. And they will find no pleasure in that.

Any event in your life, therefore, that lifts you into a fuller awareness of My Being brings happiness to you. Such an occurrence elicits from you a physical, mental, emotional, and spiritual reaction of happiness. It is always some combination of them in varying degrees, and it is sustained only as long as you respond to the greater degree of My Light. Since I eternally dwell in the balanced Polarity of My Law, I Am perfect Happiness. Happiness is inherent in My Light. Hence, all who live in My Light abide in My Happiness. If you do not constantly reside in My Happiness, you do not partake wholly of My Light.

Accordingly, as long as there is any unbalance in the Polarity of My Light in your soul, any happiness that comes into your life will never be complete nor satisfy you entirely because deep within you, in the

inner recesses of your Being, there is an innate knowing of the perfect Happiness that resides in Me and
a subconscious awareness, if not a conscious one,
that it is not yet achieved in your consciousness.
Remember, too, this inner sense of perfection that
you have is derived from My Presence within you,
and your desires for My Happiness are My Desires
for complete expression through you for My Use.

To the extent that you distort My Desires by negative response to My Light into the unbalanced action
of your human desires, they take on those destructive characteristics and qualities. As a result, when
any worldly desires are gratified, they also bring their
own imperfect happiness to you; and although they
are never fully satisfied, you can live even for lifetimes reveling in the satiation they engender. But in
time, as your soul indulges in their fulfillment, they
gradually begin to wane in the pleasure they provide
you. Often, you will indulge your soul deeper in
them, still hoping to find true happiness there until,
finally, either from the pain caused by the negativity of the events, the realization of the futility of
following such a negative course, or both, you turn
and face My Light. You hear the beckoning call of
My Still, Small Voice, and then you begin to return
to Me.

In this greater realization of My Presence, you
respond more to My Light, which gives birth into
your life its own measure of happiness. According

to the illumination and readiness of your soul, you discern My Desires in this greater Light. At first, you may nourish them falteringly, hesitantly, and only occasionally; but as they grow in your subconcious awareness, they become firmly and enduringly established. Always be ready and willing to give them up, however, because sooner or later, to the extent they are not yet of *My Pure Light*, you will find that they, too, are not equivalent to the vision of happiness you see in your awareness of Me. As you rise in spiritual consciousness, you will continuously realize an ever-truer conception of My Happiness; and each time you do, you will want to nurture your desire for *it* and let the previous one fade away until the perfect image finally comes into the full view of your spiritual perception.

At whatever time this occurs in your life, root it permanently in the desires of your soul, remembering that your desire to know My Happiness is another facet of your love for Me. Then you will have made the full turn to My Light. When you entirely accept My Pure Desire as your desire for the fulfillment of My Purpose through you in its perfect spiritual expression, then, and only then, can you know My True Happiness—the ultimate accomplishment in your soul of the full consciousness of My Presence and My Light.

Your life is ceaselessly evolving. On the frontier of that evolution is the constant achievement of an increasingly higher awareness of My Light. When you experience this growth, you feel happiness. Yet people all over the world mistakenly believe that the acquisition of material and sensuous needs and wants, by themselves, can bring My True Happiness. Your past history and present events are filled with examples of those who have sought and those who still seek to find happiness in wealth, power, position, pleasure, fame, and other similar ways. The masses of mankind clamor to satisfy such personal appetites, placing them before My Desires and My Love for the Spiritual Life that resides in the innermost recesses of their own souls. Even though they have been told numerous times, and countless instances have unequivocally demonstrated to them that none of these lower urges, in themselves, ever bring My Happiness into their lives, many of them still think, expect, and fully believe that the attainment of their personal, material aspirations alone will make them happy. Some may deny this even to themselves, but the courses of their worldly lives tell a different story. They follow the inclinations of the negative desire patterns they have established in their subconscious minds, not the deeper, inner Desires coming from My Presence within them.

Let Me put this in more specific terms. As a soul is born into physical form, he immediately sets about to satisfy his needs and wants. The baby cries for milk, for warmth, for comfort, and for love. During the time he gets them, he is content. While he grows older, the dimensions of his world expand, and his necessities and desires increase commensurately. He enjoys walking, running, playing, talking, eating, and socializing, among many other things. When such activities as these are sufficiently satisfied, he usually becomes what is often described as a happy child.

As a youth, while he further matures into adulthood, still more needs and wants emerge into his life. His physical, mental, and emotional appetites come into full bloom. He is glad when his affections are returned and elated and thrilled when he finds his lifelong mate. His children bring much gratification and fulfillment into his life. Throughout his lifetime, he is pleased with all of his successes. According to his ambitions and abilities, he acquires a home, a vocation, and employment to help him achieve his dreams of a good and happy life. His desires may even lead him to aspire to be a great leader in his chosen field, to amass a huge fortune, and to become famous for his talents and skills—all for some noble ideal. The satisfaction of these accomplishments are very rewarding to him.

Or, following in the lower, more negative vibrations of his consciousness, such an individual may find great pleasure in the overindulgence of his physical senses, in sexual promiscuity and the wasting of his life force, in using alcohol and drugs to excess, in gluttony, in the abuse of his power, his fortune, and his fame, or in many other ways. The motivations of the average person, however, lie somewhere in between these extremes.

Consider the life of anyone you know, or look at your history and find yet more; and you will discover that, with considerable modifications to fit each individual, whoever you choose will display some kind of similar pattern of living as I have just described in his attempt to fulfill his desires and needs and in his search for happiness. And as you look into your own life, you will find it there too. Thus, it is clear that everyone is seeking My Happiness in his own degree of spiritual awareness, each in his own unique way. Some are deeply engrossed in destructive vibrations. For the majority, their lives are an assorted mixture of positive and negative expression. There are only a few, therefore, who have directed their desires solely toward the achievement of My Happiness, those who have keenly felt My Presence and clearly heard My Voice.

With their minds and their emotions being held in the grip of the negative force of their own creation, the masses of mankind still do not really know the truth of My Presence; they have not, even yet, actually discovered the joyful, silent promptings of My Still, Small Voice. Now as before, they retain their faith in the unreal appearance of the unbalanced Polarity of My Light. Moreover, they will continue to follow their negative, personal desires until their souls mature enough to enable them to recognize My Reality and turn to Me instead.

With great patience, I await that time when they can sense My Presence enough to heed My Call. Although it may not be for centuries for some of them, when they do want the real Life of My Light, I will be there ready to show them the Way, even as I Am doing for you now; for as you now know, I Am with them always, just as I Am with you. At that joyous time, I will gradually lead them into the greater awareness of My Desires and of My Impersonal, Divine Love, lifting them in spiritual consciousness until I have perfect expression in and through them in the physical plane. As they learn to accept My Desires as their own, they, too, will find their true Happiness in Me to be My Happiness through them, all to the glory of God in the spiritual Unity of My Light.

Looking from another perspective of My Life, it can be seen that the degree of maturity of the consciousness of anyone also affects his human search for happiness. A baby may laugh with glee one moment and cry with displeasure the next. Its happiness is determined by its needs or wants of the instant and the extent to which they are filled. As he grows older, he can be happy and rejoice in the anticipation of the achievement of a desire he expects to experience in an hour or so. In the vivid, mental awareness of its imminent reality, his thoughts of the event persist in his mind from the moment of their conception. Consequently, the occasion has its own genuine existence in his mind before he brings it forth into the physical plane, and he revels in it. Thus, he is happy, not only during the occurrence, itself, but also while he waits for the future incident to happen.

While a person's age continues to increase and he becomes yet more mature, his capacity to extend this time span between the inception of a desire and its fulfillment, during which he can be joyous in the prospect of its attainment, continuously grows larger. So a child can be joyful for a pleasant occasion that is going to happen the next day or, perhaps, the next week; and an older youth, even the following year. Once he fully matures, he can be happy while he endures yet longer periods of waiting for the accomplishment of his desires, even when their attainment requires severe self-discipline, struggle, pain, and suffering. For example, he may travail for years to master some skills or certain knowledge that will bring to him the happiness which that greater expression of My Light will enable him to have, such as studying and practicing to learn the proficiencies of an accomplished athlete, artist, or scholar.

For someone to be a Master in the making, however, his soul must become still more mature than what is usually considered to be a mature person in your world. In the anticipation of Spiritual Mastery and of My Happiness that it brings, he conceives in his mind the perfect image of My Reality and My Presence within himself. And as he lives within My Law, he constantly holds his attention in the joyous awareness of that image until it is completely established in his entire consciousness, until it is permanently imprinted in his soul. While he continuously lives in his mental perception of My Perfection, he enjoys his own degree of My Happiness, which, in his greater maturity, can extend over an entire lifetime or even for many lifetimes. The average person's spiritual perspective, endurance, and faith would not survive such a rigorous test of happiness. However, for him, this inner joy persists even in the midst of his struggle with the negative conditions he finds in his own life and any suffering they may bring as he rises in conciousness in My Light and as he patiently, steadily, and knowingly works to achieve the fulfillment of his desires, which are My Desires, for Mastery. Once achieved, he abides completely in My Happiness as he lives in My Eternity.

So, of course, it should be your objective, as a student on the Path of My Light, to seek My Happiness. Let the flame of your desire burn fiercely for it. Know that in searching for My Happiness, you must look to find Me. It comes to you only as you come to Me in conscious and subconscious awareness. As you desire a greater expression of My Light, the attainment of it requires a purging, correcting, and strengthening of many things in your soul. In the process of that cleansing, your experiences may cause you varying degrees of suffering as you wrest from your soul persistent negative patterns that do not want to go and discipline yourself to rebuild perfect ones to take their places.

Yet the elimination of those undesirable qualities and their replacement with My Light brings a release and freedom in your consciousness from the limitations of their lower vibrations. With this achievement, your soul comes into a greater knowing of My Happiness. Hence, it is apparent that My Happiness is born even out of the suffering of your soul and the pains of your life. And you can experience it only in the process of the removal of the negative conditions causing them and in the correction of the unbalanced Polarity of My Light. However, this is the price that you must pay, as it is for every soul, if you truly desire to find My Happiness by lifting yourself in consciousness into the perfect expression of My Light and into the full awareness of My Presence.

CHAPTER XIX

My Mind and Body

You now understand, dear seeker of the Higher Life, that I Am you and you are Me. It only logically follows, then, that My Mind is your mind and My Body is your body. Yes, we are truly One, although you fully realize that we are not yet One in consciousness. It is important for you to clearly comprehend, therefore, just how it can be that we are One at the same time that we are not united in spiritual consciousness. In order for Me to enable you to know that, it is necessary to describe to you in some detail the composition of My Anatomy, which is also your anatomy, and to explain how it functions.

I have only one Body and one Mind, but there are three phases of My Body and three phases of My Mind. You are only too acutely aware of your physical phase of body and conscious phase of mind as your physical senses dominate in your perception of

My Life. It is the physical phase of body in which you live in your material world, and it is the conscious phase of mind with which you think, reason, and direct your activities and affairs in determining the course of your life throughout each incarnation. It is this phase of body and mind in which you gain the needed experiences in the physical plane to enable you to grow into the ever-greater awareness of My Being.

Since your conscious phase of mind, through your physical senses, can sense only your physical body and your material world, you have come to accept them as the only reality of My Life that you truly know to exist. For this reason, it becomes a revelation to you to be told that your physical body and conscious mind are merely one of three phases of My Body and Mind. And especially does it seem strange to you to hear that your material world as you know it is the least real of the three.

Heretofore, you have not even really known of My Existence within your Temple of My Light; and to the extent that you cannot entirely accept what I Am telling you now, your materiality still blinds you to the awareness of My Reality. You will have to accept in faith the Truth of My Presence within you until you can rise enough in spiritual consciousness to become fully aware of My Essence and My True

Reality that dwells within your very soul. As I have said before, only then will you verily know the Truth of My Being, your heritage in My Light.

In addition to your awareness of the material phase of your body and mind, you do have some conscious cognition of your subconscious phase of mind as you experience the many mental and emotional habit-patterns that are established in your consciousness. You remember your dreams, and you recognize your faith and fears, your loves and hates, your strengths and weaknesses, and the many other traits that appear to be inborn in your soul; although now you know they are all learned. So by this time you have some perception that your subconscious awareness is simply the expression of your living soul. You realize that your soul *is* your subconscious phase of mind.

Yet it may seem stranger still for you to learn that you have a phase of body for your subconscious phase of mind. However, as you reflect upon this concept, it should seem only natural that you do. To describe it differently, your soul is another phase of My Mind and Body. Your soul is made up of your subconscious phase of mind and astral phase of body. They both are composed of astral substance—substance of the astral plane of My Life, a plane of higher frequencies of My Light than the physical. Of course, you cannot know of them through your physical senses because they can sense only physical substance, not astral substance. Since your physical senses presently dominate your consciousness, you have little conscious awareness of the reality of your soul except by means of the sensitivity of your feelings—your emotions—and their patterns you have built into your consciousness. Herein is found the basic urges of mankind, positive and negative; and they are present in every person, each according to how he has established them in his soul. As discussed before, from them is derived the human struggle of good and evil. However, to the extent that you cannot perceive the reality of your astral phase of body and subconscious phase of mind— your soul—you will also have to accept in faith what I Am explaining to you here until you can grow into a deeper spiritual responsiveness to My Light.

Even the most depraved of souls have some awareness of My Reality, however slight it may be. When a sufficient measure of the negative expression of their own misguided creations returns to them to be redeemed, the most confirmed atheists or debased characters will invariably cry out in their suffering: Oh God! My God! Help me! Help me! The great majority of mankind, however, sees but a glimmer of the radiant brilliance of My Light that abides mostly hidden in the depth of their materialistic souls. Yet, it *is there*; and each in his own small degree, according to his spiritual consciousness, *knows* that it is there. Thus, only a relatively few have come to realize to any large extent the fuller Light of My Presence within them. Still, be certain that you understand that My Light is coming forth into the hearts and minds of all the people of the earth, gradually, continuously, and surely. In the dawn of a New Age, it is coming forth into the world, just as the sunlight silently, steadily, and gloriously inches its way into the morning of another day.

But presently, the awareness of the physical senses of the masses is so predominant in their consciousness that, for most, the reality of My Presence seems vague and indistinct. In proportion to his own response to My Light, each of them discerns his own version of My Reality. Some believe that I Am the Spirit in the wind, the rain, or the sun. Others conceive Me to be in a mountain, in the sea, or in some great tree. Yet others believe that I Am in the form of an animal or a human being, making graven images of these forms and worshiping them. And there are those who conceive me to be in some abstract form. They look without to find Me. Few really look within themselves even though I have told them throughout the ages that I Am within them. When they do, the obscurity of their darkened vision too often does not reveal to them the reality that I Am there. Seeing nothing, they turn without again to find Me.

Yes, it is true that I Am everywhere you and all mankind have looked to find Me; remember, I Am All there is. Yet, you can *reach* Me and discover the reality of My Being and of My Presence *only* within the depth of your own soul. I have told you this Truth so many times and in so many ways because it is so important for you to realize it and for the reason that this realization has been so difficult for the human mind to achieve in conscious awareness.

So if it seems incredible for you to realize that I Am within you, when I tell you further that you have a spiritual phase of Body and Mind more real than your physical or astral phases of body and conscious or subconscious phases of mind, you may turn away in utter disbelief. You may see little or nothing to substantiate such a concept of My Reality. Yet it is true. When you see Me in such dim light of your soul, it is again necessary that you accept in faith what I Am relating to you herein to the extent that you cannot perceive the reality of My Presence. Then, as you follow in My Light, I can make Myself known to you—that I Am you and that you are Me.

Follow closely while I explain. Your subconscious phase of mind and astral phase of body are within the center of every cell of your physical phase of body. In the same way, your spiritual phase of Mind and Body are within the center of every cell of your astral phase of body. So, your spiritual and astral phases of mind and body are both within your physical phase of body; in the order just described, each is within the other. And since you know that the intelligence of God is in everything, everywhere, you can easily understand that My Mind is in every cell of each phase of your body, which is My Body, directing its every function.

Now, for one phase of My Body to be within the other does not mean that it is merely inside of it, although that is true; but, it is within it on a higher plane of existence. Within the physical plane, the astral plane exists, which is a higher plane of My Life, a plane of more tenuous substance than the physical. Thus, it is present within it in a higher frequency of My Light. Similarly, within the astral plane is a yet higher plane of My Life, the spiritual plane. It, in turn, is a plane of still more tenuous substance than the astral. Therefore, it likewise exists within the astral plane in an even higher frequency of My Light than the astral. In identical fashion, the three phases of your body and mind have their being together, one within the other as described above, but each on a different plane of My Life.

You might liken these relationships of the planes of My Being to measuring cups, one within the other, or to free oxygen in water, which is contained between the water molecules. Yet these analogies do not portray the true concept of how the three phases of My Body abide together, one within the other, because such approximations depict only physical associations, while the affinity of the phases of My Body occurs in the different planes of My Life. Hence, though these similarities may be of some help in your understanding this concept, you may need to spend a considerable amount of time in Meditation before you can fully comprehend how substances of the different planes of My Life, the three phases of My Body, can exist together in the same point of space at the same time.

Let Me describe the relationship of the phases of your body to you in another way to help you to understand it further. These phases of body and mind do not exist together in different points of space as you conceive things to be in your physical plane. Rather, they abide in different degrees of vibration or frequency of My Light; but all three of them are in the same point of space at the same moment of time. Of course, you know that it is impossible for two or more material objects in the physical plane alone to be in the same point of space at the same time. However, this does not hold true for objects composed of substance of different planes. So it is only a natural occurrence for the three phases of your body and mind, each existing on a different plane of My Life, to be an integral part of each other, as one, in the same point of physical space, the finer substance within the courser substance.

These are completely new concepts for the human mind that has an orientation only to the physical plane as most people do, and you may wonder why I Am telling you these things in such detail. The reason is very simple. With this emphasis upon the Oneness of the three phases of My Body and Mind, you may be able to perceive more clearly how intimately close I Am to you at all times. I Am closer than your breath, and all you need to do to come into the realization of My Presence is to lift yourself spiritually into the vibrations of My Divine, Impersonal Love.

My Spiritual Phase of Body, which is always perfect as God is perfect, is the mold by which your astral phase of body is formed except for the imperfections you have established in your soul, your astral body and subconscious mind, due to the unbalance of the Polarity of My Light that you have created therein. In like manner, your astral phase of body is the die from which your physical phase of body is cast, the latter taking on all of your soul's imperfections as well as its perfections—all of its negative and positive traits.

Each phase of body is an intrinsic and inseparable part of the others, existing together in the same point of space at the same time. Yet, each abides in a different plane of My Life—in different frequencies of My Light. As you develop your astral and spiritual senses, these phases of your body will gradually come into your conscious awareness. Then, you will recognize their Oneness at the same moment that you perceive their different phases as they exist together, for you will have come into the Oneness of My Light *in consciousness* with Me.

So even though we are One, and you understand that, you are not consciously aware of it now because you are living in the lower vibrations of the unbalanced Polarity of My Light. When you follow the guidance of My Still, Small Voice and live within My Spiritual Law, correcting the negative conditions in your soul that you have established there by means of negative living in your past and present incarnations, then you will lift your soul into harmony with the perfection of My Vibrations and into the peace of My Love. At that time, we will not only be One in phases of Body and Mind, but also One in spiritual consciousness. In so becoming, you will enable Me to raise you up into the glory of My Light, transforming you into a Spiritual Master and giving Me perfect expression through you into all the planes of My Life.

CHAPTER XX

My Guiding Presence

You and I are an intrinsic part of one another, you being My Creation, an extension of Myself into the physical plane, and I being your Creator, an individualized expression of God, progressing in the evolution of spiritual unfoldment into eternity. This message I Am giving you herein is as ageless as Life, itself, but the masses of humanity on earth have little or no real appreciation of the significance of what it means for them to enter into the full realization of My Reality and My Light within them. The mere mental concept that I Am within you, with all of its profound importance, pales into obscurity when compared to the actual consummation of your consciousness into My Consciousness.

Therefore, as the New Age enters and as humanity recognizes the Truth of My Reality, the realm of Spirit will become a new frontier for mankind to explore and master and the last frontier for him as a human being. For in its conquest, he will learn that he is required to master himself first; and in achieving that, he will find it necessary to surrender his will completely to My Will and permit Me, thereafter, to guide his life in all things. The reality of My Spirit will increasingly come forth into his awareness until My Presence is as vivid in his consciousness as his material body and the physical plane. Beyond this frontier, he will emerge a Master of My Light, rising above the human into the Divine. You now understand that this is the Destiny of all mankind; and he is carried along in the upward spiraling current of the evolving cycles of My Life as My Spiritual Law unfolds into its ever-greater expression of My Light. In its own time, this movement in the human consciousness will dominate all the activities of mankind on earth.

Since it is your certain Destiny to rise into My Spiritual Consciousness and inherit the glories of My Kingdom, it is to your every advantage to fully cooperate with My Great Law in every possible way that you can in order to lift yourself into the greater expression of My Divine Love. Any delays you may cause will only result in the increased suffering of your soul, for they become added obstacles that you must remove from your Path, making it harder for you to rise in spiritual consciousness. Hence, you incur a greater karmic debt, and you will be required to pay it at some later time when the vibrations of My Light become more intensified as the cycle of My Spiritual Law spirals upward. Yes, get into the full flow and move with the current of My Love that carries you into your Destiny of Spiritual Mastery even now. Never resist for a moment its powerful Urge—My Desire for your spiritual unfoldment.

You know, then, that as you respond more and more to My Light, you acquire a keener spiritual sensitivity that reveals to you an even fuller awareness of My Presence within you, in your life, and in the world in which you live. This enables you to hear more readily and easily and to interpret more correctly My Still, Small Voice as I guide you in positive expression in your everyday living. At the same time, you are more effectively able to recognize and reject the negative voice of the unbalanced Polarity of My Light in your own soul and in the world that will always attempt to mislead you and even lure you away from your Path of My Light if you would permit it.

Thus you become increasingly better able to distinguish between the Positive Force of My Light and the negative force of darkness in any condition, circumstance, situation, person, or thing as they seek admission into your life each day. It is essential that you develop your discriminative skills to the highest degree that it is possible for you to achieve if you expect to be able to walk your Path of My Light safely and not get lost in the maze of the negative vibrations that you will have to meet and master in yourself and in the world as you grow spiritually. The Way is narrow and the Gate is strait that enters into My Kingdom, and there are only a few who find it.

However, if you carefully follow what I Am revealing to you herein, attentively listen to Me as I guide your life each day, persistently develop your ability to differentiate vividly between Positive and negative expression, and consistently train yourself to accept only the positive action of My Love into your life at all times, you will constantly abide in My Divine Guidance and Protection. Then you will be able to travel your Path of My Light safely, avoiding all the detours and pitfalls that await the soul who does not properly prepare himself for this Journey of his life and who is careless in living the Spiritual Laws of My Light, in listening to My Inner Guidance, and in heeding its directions.

Always remember, you can never reach Spiritual Mastery alone: it is only in and through Me that you can attain it, and it is I who lift you up into My Spirit when you live within My Law and in My Love. I even give to you your greater spiritual sensitiveness that reveals to you your deeper awareness of My Presence. Fully recognize that I do it all through you when you open yourself to My Light; you are but the instrument for My Use. Constantly live in the humility of this realization of My Truth, although you recognize that you are an indispensable part of My Being and that I cannot fulfill My Desire for the attainment of your Spiritual Mastery except through you. I can attain My Glory through you only as you achieve your Glory through Me—another example of Our Oneness in My Being.

With your spiritual growth and your greater spiritual sensitivity that it brings to you, you develop a sharper spiritual insight. My Light increases in your consciousness and enables you to *see* deeper into My Reality; and to the extent that your soul fully partakes of that Light, then you actually *experience* that Reality. It *becomes* your higher consciousness. It is your mind that perceives and, in perceiving, experiences.

You are accustomed to thinking of your brain as your mind, but it is really an instrument of My Mind, which is also your mind. With this instrument, your human brain, you view your material world by means of the impressions received by your physical senses, which are vibrational emanations radiating from material substance. So you generally recognize that you can perceive your material world only through your physical organs of sense, and this is true.

I have told you, however, that your Superconscious phase of Mind—My Mind—and your subconscious phase of mind, as well as your Spiritual phase of Body and your astral phase of body, exist in every cell of your physical phase of body. I have further explained that My Intelligence and My Light are contained in every form of substance, which, therefore, also fill your mind and body. You understand, too, that your emotions or your feelings are an expression of My Light and My Life in and through you.

So as you come to be increasingly more sensitive to My Light and to My Guidance, every cell of your body becomes able to sense the finer vibrations of My Life. Their sensing faculty becomes more pronounced in your consciousness, and they become *sensors* similar to the function of your physical senses, able to receive any impressions of vibrations that affect them as you live in your world. They can sense vibrations coming from any plane of My Being to which they have become sufficiently sensitive for such reception. Hence, their activity is not limited to the physical plane as are your physical senses.

The current of My Life—My Energy, My Life Force, My Love—is constantly coursing through every cell of your body, giving it its energy, its vitality, and its strength. It is this same Life Force that gives to you your feelings or your emotions; and this very current, which you also recognize as your nerve energy, carries the messages of your physical senses to your brain for its interpretation of your material world. As My Light increases in your consciousness and all the cells of your body become sensors, this current, in like manner, also carries impressions to your brain that they receive from any plane of My Being to enable you to perceive and comprehend their meaning. So it is your emotions—My Life—by means of which you sense your outer and inner worlds of My Being, now and as you grow into an ever-increasing awareness of their presence.

Accordingly, as your physical sense organs send their impressions to your brain to perceive their messages, so also do the cells of your body transmit their sensations to your brain for interpretation, all using My Life Force or Nerve Energy. As you become sensitive to the higher vibrations of My Light, therefore, all the cells of your body are able to sense vibrations coming from any plane of My Life; and your brain is able to detect and correctly interpret them according to the degree of spiritual consciousness you have attained. As a result, you develop a conscious awareness, not only of the physical plane which you now have, but also of the higher planes of My Life, as far as your spiritual sensitivity enables you to perceive. Thus, you can see, hear, feel, smell, and taste on those planes as well as you can on the physical plane, as you presently are able to do. With spiritual unfoldment, your finer faculties blossom forth.

As a consequence of this new awareness, you begin to *live* on the inner planes of My Being as naturally as you have customarily lived on the physical plane. You are able to experience these higher Planes, moreover, just as vividly as you presently do your physical plane. Then you more fully realize how limited is your present concept of My Life that you have acquired from your conscious awareness of your physical plane alone. You begin to know some of My Worlds within your world. You commence to see the full cycles of some of the Spiritual Laws that you cannot presently witness, such as the effects of causes or the causes of effects, only one part of which you find in your current incarnation. In such manner, with your expanded consciousness, you are able to perceive many things that you cannot even sense until you seek the greater Light of My Love and lift yourself into the spiritual consciousness that will permit you to partake of the higher Life of My Being.

To ascend into such spiritual vibrations, however, requires a thorough cleansing of your soul so that the dross of the negative material world is washed clean from your subconscious mind and astral body, leaving only the purity of My Spirit therein. It is, furthermore, in this heightened awareness of My Love that you begin not only to recognize My Voice and My Presence, but to realize that My Voice *is* your voice and My Presence *is* your presence—to grasp the fact that we are One. This is the most precious experience that a traveler on the Path of My Light can have because it assures him that I Am able to guide his every step along his Way to Spiritual Mastery, enabling him to successfully pass the many trials, tests, and initiations he will be required to meet as he rises to Me in spiritual consciousness. Here too, moreover, in this greater awareness of My Love, the experiences of the higher Realms, resulting from your deeper spiritual sensitivity, are vastly insignificant when compared to the invaluable importance—the indispensibility—of achieving the cognition of My Guiding Presence within you, because it is the only way you can successfully follow Me and walk in My Light. To attain Spiritual Mastery, you must be able to hear and willing to heed My Still, Small Voice.

In this finer frequency of My Light, you feel the intensified power of My Life in every cell of your body as you steadfastly abide in the deeper awareness of My Presence. With your attention centered with Me as you follow My Guidance, you withdraw it from the mass-mind consciousness of your world. You become no longer dependent upon the negative thought-force of humanity. You assert and maintain your own true identity—My Identity through you—and your God-given individuality, no more fettered and trammelled by the dominating influences of the unreal world of materiality and by the bondage of its enticements and limitations.

As you train your mind to respond wholly to the positive expression of My Light, you see all conditions of your life bend to your will as you live according to My Will and to My Law. You fully realize the power of mind, not only over matter, but over all forms of all substance on all planes of My Being. Hence, in surrendering your will to My Will—of your own free will—you are able to attain the perfect freedom of the expression of your own individuality as you realize the complete awareness of your Oneness with Me. And all of this you achieve by recognizing, hearing, obeying, and entirely trusting My Guiding Presence within the very depth of your own Being.

Able to Hear
Willing to Heed

CHAPTER XXI

Your Path of My Light

Though there is only one Way to My Kingdom and though it is narrow and the Gate is strait, the Path of each wayfarer along Life's Highroad has a uniqueness all its own. As no two souls are exactly alike, neither are their Paths of My Light completely the same, each freely and fully learning to express his true personality, which is a reflection of his own Divine Individuality. So everyone must walk his different Path that leads him to his Destiny, according to the needs and desires of his soul and the will of his mind.

You know, dear aspirant of the Higher Life, I give you complete freedom to direct the course of your life, entirely respecting your personal identity and even your free will. This enables you to flower forth unrestricted into the full bloom of My Creative Originality. Yet as you proceed along the Way of My Light, you wholly preserve your distinctiveness, losing nothing of your innate selfhood. Furthermore, in so doing, you develop it to its peak of perfection because I Am Perfection; and you know that My Individuality is your individuality since we are One.

Realizing this Oneness, always remember that there is only one Way to Spiritual Mastery: *I Am the only Way*. You must walk with Me in My Light and live within My Spiritual Law if you truly desire to attain the real freedom of your soul that you profess to seek. Why do I repeat this Truth? It is because few there are, still, who veritably hear My Voice and the message it brings; and having heard, many of them do not even yet know My Reality. They do not heed My Call nor do they really realize My Presence. Their souls waken slowly, lethargically, and falteringly, still spellbound by the mesmeric appearances and the resultant conceptions of their material lives. The beginning of the New Age is upon them; and as it progresses, the process of their unfoldment is being quickened. By its powerful influence upon their budding souls, My Light will soon flood into their hearts and minds, enabling the consciousness of My Spirit to begin to enter therein and take its rightful place. They must be prepared to receive Me.

In following the Path of My Light toward Spiritual Mastery, your mind and your endeavors must always be directed toward the positive expression of My Love at all times and under all circumstances. Strict self-discipline is paramount to your success in correcting all negative impressions in your soul and meeting positively all inharmonious conditons of the world that My Spiritual Law brings before you to be redeemed and to give you the opportunity to learn the lessons they have to teach you. Spiritually speaking, then, a successful life is not measured in material terms of traditional worldly standards of success, such as income, job status, education, social standing, etc. Rather, it is determined by how well you learn the spiritual lessons My Law brings before you and the extent to which you live in My Light.

The spiritually successful person is one who carefully listens to My Inner Voice and religiously follows My Directions. He is one who lives continuously within My Law to the best of his knowledge and ability. His motive and intention are always to make the positive response to everything that affects his life. He conscientiously practices all the virtues. The flame of his desire for the higher Life burns fiercely in his soul. He is modestly always trying to lift himself spiritually and to awaken those around him to an awareness of My Spirit within them. The Silence and Meditation are routine practices in his life; and he makes every effort to take his Silence with him at all times, wherever he goes and whatever he does.

The person who is a spiritual success may or may not be what the world calls successful. He may be high or low, rich or poor, loved or hated, and known or unknown. And although he may stumble, fall, or even fail in all his endeavors so that it may appear to an onlooker that he is losing instead of gaining in his struggle of life, if he is doing his utmost in every way that he knows to balance the Positive and Negative Polarity of My Light in his life, carefully following My Guidance, then he is an astounding success. He is passing his spiritual tests with flying colors. Any semblance of failure, material or spiritual, simply becomes for him stepping-stones upward into the spiritual Life of My Light. He may often be making more spiritual progress than someone who appears to have his life well in hand.

Here again, the outer appearance can be very deceiving. Spiritual growth is an inner development of your soul and cannot be reliably monitored from without. The criteria are: what are the experiences My Law is bringing to you, positive or negative, easy or difficult; what is the strength of your soul; and what is the extent to which you are applying My Law and My Guidance to lift yourself into My Light. When you do your very best, God asks no more; and you are always victorious when you positively respond to My Life, no matter what the outcome may seem to be.

The only way you can fail spiritually is when you cease to try to come to My Light—when you give up the effort; and then you only delay your progress because it is your Destiny to reach Spiritual Mastery some day. So the successful one is he who never quits, who tries again and again, endlessly, until he finally achieves his goal; and this is true for all endeavors of life, material and spiritual.

In spiritual training, however, it is especially important for you to develop an undaunted perseverance because you are continuously living in faith in an unseen world; and you are working with effects, the causes of which you may not know, as well as with causes, the effects of which you may not see. Therefore, in creating or correcting anything in your life, it is essential that you keep at it until you are triumphant, even if it takes years, a lifetime, or more to accomplish it. Be reminded that in the spiritual response to My Light, you live in eternity, not just a lifetime; yet it is necessary that you make every minute count.

Hence as you steadfastly shape your life to fit My Spiritual Mold, your Path continuously leads you into the more brilliant radiance of My Light. As you receive My Truth, consistently apply it to your life in your everyday thinking, feeling, speaking, and acting. You know it is your conscious phase of mind that trains or conditions your subconscious phase of mind. When you invariably heed My Guidance and live in the positive action of My Light, all of the impressions you give to your soul are always constructive and good. As a result, your conscious and subconscious phases of mind work harmoniously together with My Superconscious Phase of Mind,

each constantly responding to the same vibrations—
like desires and concepts. Because of this consistent,
positive conditioning, your soul, knowing precisely
what you want, brings to you the exact fulfillment
of all your creations from My Divine Supply.

However, when you inconsistently obey My Law,
living your life according to My Truth at one moment and following some untruth the next, you are
implanting into your subconscious mind two or
more conflicting desires. When you continue to
establish such irregular patterns in your soul, you
confuse it. Receiving discordant directions, it does
not know what you want. So it either produces
nothing for you, or it brings to you a distorted, imperfect creation at best.

How does your soul do this? As My Energy flows
through you and out into your world, an electromagnetic field of spiritual energy is generated in
your soul. It is always there, abiding with you at all
times. This energy is the light of your soul; it comprises your aura. It functions in you spiritually similar to the way that an iron electromagnet works in
the material plane. According to the frequencies of
My Light that you permit to flow through you as a
result of the thoughts you hold in your mind, conscious and subconscious, the spiritual magnetic attraction they produce in your soul draws into your
life conditions of like vibrations, positive or negative and strong or weak, just as magnetized iron at-

tracts objects of iron to itself. This is My Spiritual Law, and this radiation of your soul is My Love, My Life, and My Light. It reaches into infinity to bring to you the fulfillment of your every desire.

Hence, you draw to yourself and into your life, as all do, the consequences of the spiritual awareness you have attained at any given time. Therefore, your consciousness, having its own electromagnetic field of *spiritual* energy, attracts to you its own degree of positive and negative experiences—its own quality and quantity of your friends, your wealth, your personal charm, your abilities, your vocational skills, your health, your happiness, your spirituality, your successes, your failures, your strengths, your weaknesses, etc. Yes, My Spiritual Law works out in your life in as exacting a way as any law of physics or chemistry in the material plane in which you live.

Of course, then, as one who aspires for Spiritual Mastery, it becomes your responsibility to follow My Inner Guidance and to live in My Love at all times in order to achieve the highest consciousness of which you are capable. In so doing, the electromagnetic attraction of your soul draws to you the greatest spiritual and material success that is possible at any given period or phase of your spiritual unfoldment. All of this results because you become consistent in your constructive thinking, speaking, feeling, and acting; and your subconscious mind receives only those positive impressions. Since they are all unvaryingly positive, your soul knows precisely what you want and brings your needs and desires into manifestation in your life at the right time and in their own degree of perfection.

I Am able to reveal to you higher Truths for you to establish in your consciousness as you continue to experience the finer vibrations of My Light. When you constantly apply them to your daily living of My Law, desiring their fulfillment in your life, they, in turn, begin to become a part of the electromagnetic field of spiritual energy of your soul, establishing there the consciousness of their reality and attracting to you the manifest expression of that reality. As a consequence, your spiritual and material successes become more positive, more frequent, and more enduring.

Moreover, when you persist in the application of these Truths in your life as you walk your Path of My Light, you keep lifting yourself into the greater awareness of My Love and into the realization of the increased Divine Supply that it draws into your life, both spiritually and materially. Finally, you make your complete Ascension into My Light and fully attain your desire for Spiritual Mastery. Thus you enable Me to fulfill My Desire in you for our Union in spiritual consciousness. You become a perfect success in My Light in every way on every plane, and you inherit the abundance of My Unlimited Supply for eternity.

CHAPTER XXII

Your Path and My Peace

In all the foregoing chapters, you have learned many things about Me and about My Light. By now, you should have a very clear comprehension about who I Am, where you will find Me, and how you can reach Me. To your own degree of spiritual awareness, you have recognized the reality of My Presence within you in the very depth of your soul. In order to help you more fully realize your Divine Heritage, I have emphasized to you your Destiny: to unite with Me in consciousness, to make your Ascension into My Light, and to achieve Spiritual Mastery. Hence, you understand that you and I are One and that this concept of My Truth is of paramount importance for you who wish to travel your Path of My Light, seeking to find My Peace.

Title

I have described to you My Still, Small Voice and told you how you can always recognize it. I have also cautioned you about the negative voice that constantly tries to mislead you and lure you away from My Guidance and My Light. I have talked to you about the Silence and Meditation, detailing for you what they are and how to use them. So now you understand the basic background that you need in order to be able to enter the Silence more effectively and then carry it with you at all times. Additionally, you know how to properly breathe in order to achieve greater physical, mental, emotional, and spiritual health.

You comprehend something of My Truth and how you should use your heart and head, working harmoniously together, to know it and follow it. Moreover, I have told you what Spiritual Mastery is, what you need to do to achieve it, and where and how you can get the necessary training for it. You have some cognition of the nature of My Being and of the Positive and Negative Polarity of My Light. Furthermore, I have revealed to you what some of My Spiritual Laws are and the importance of learning them and living them in order to attain ever-higher levels of spiritual consciousness.

I have explained much of the nature of My Love and its degrees as they are found in the world. You realize that it is your responsibility to aspire to its highest form—My Divine, Impersonal Love. You are also aware of important facets of My Faith and how it is interwoven with My Truth as you seek to find it in your upward spiral toward My Light. And you know that in your search for My Happiness, it will ever elude you until you rise in consciousness into the purity of My Love. In addition, I have disclosed to you and carefully described the three phases of your Mind and Body. You understand their functions and how they work together as One, and you recognize the importance of your emotions in enabling your mind to perceive the reality of My Being.

Besides all of this, I have pointed out to you how your Path of My Light is unique to your own identity and yet how you, as everyone, have only one Way that you can go to reach My Kingdom—only through Me and in My Light. So, inasmuch as your heart and mind have led you to learn My Truth, it is evident that you, too, search for the Peace of My Light. But are you really ready to turn away from the things of the world and follow after the guidance of My Spirit? You know that it takes much courage and fortitude to walk in My Footsteps. In their own proper time, according to My Spiritual Law, all of the carnal things of your flesh must be lifted up into My Love and transmuted into My Divinity. There is no other Way to find My Peace.

You who truly want My Spiritual Life need to cultivate all of the spiritual values—the virtues—and instill their positive qualities into your soul. Love, compassion, honesty, truth, temperance, understanding, kindness, forgiveness, patience, faith, courage, forbearance, justice, prudence, and hope are but some of them. To accomplish this, it is mandatory for you to eliminate all negative qualities from your subconscious mind and astral body until there is nothing left but My Divine Love and all of its attributes.

All fear, hate, selfishness, lust, anger, criticism, greed, worry, anxiety, jealousy, revenge, resentment, envy, impatience, intolerance, doubt, grief, deception, and any of the myriad of other negative traits that may reside in your subconscious mind must be transformed into My Impersonal Love—the Love for all of Life. It is essential that you cleanse your soul as white as snow until you have only My Love to give, not only to those you love, but to everyone, even the sinful, negative, destructive souls and any seeming enemies you may have.

Of course, it means, too, that you need to develop further physical, mental, emotional, and spiritual strength, improving your health generally, but this comes naturally as you climb the spiritual ladder of My Life, step by step. There is the process of training your mind and emotions to respond always positively to My Light and to My Love, balancing the Positive and Negative Polarities of My Being in your life.

A strong will and the ability to discipline yourself to do what you know must be done is indispensable. Still, your will and any implications of self-will must be entirely and unconditionally surrendered to God and His Will, and all of this done of your own free will. And since I Am One with God, the surrender of your will is also to My Will. Moreover, as you learn My Spiritual Laws, it is essential that you apply them in your life until you can live entirely within them every minute of every day of your life.

Yet always remember that to follow Me and to walk in your Path of My Light is just as easy as you make it. Resist not evil, but walk in the Way of My Righteousness. As a serious student of My Light, you never strive nor contend with any aspect of the negative force; neither do you ever strike back at it. You simply live within My Law and in My Light wherever or whenever the negative force enters your life. When you live in My Love, you never need to fear, for then you abide in its guidance and protection as well as in its divine supply. And I will never forsake you because, as you know, I Am always with you, even until the end of the earth— the end of your sojourn in earthly living, and beyond.

Since it is your Destiny to rise in consciousness in My Light into Oneness with Me, it seems reasonable that you would conclude that you have no other course to follow but to commence now. Whatever it takes, it needs to be done, all to the glory of God as it also glorifies Me and you. To delay only makes your life harder now and in your future because of the greater debt of negative living you will have to pay. The past is gone and the present is all you have, since the future never comes. There is no better time to start; there is no *other* time in which you can begin to follow Me. If you have already taken your place on your Path of My Light, then let us valiantly proceed together. For, united in consciousness with Me, you stand. Separated from Me, you can only fall, because then you partake of the negative force of the world—the unbalanced Polarity of My Law.

The word has been spoken. The call has been sounded to all mankind to make this turn to My Love and My Light. THE TIME IS NOW. Are you ready to walk in the greater Light of My Love? Can you feel My Inner Desire within the depth of your soul for the full expression of My Consciousness in and through you, prompting you to allow Me rightfully to take My Place in your heart and mind? Yes, if you are already following your Path of My Light, you have heard and heeded My Call. If you have not heard or if you have heard but not heeded, the circumstances of your own future rest chiefly in your hands. You are the arbiter of your soul, and you shall decide of your own free will.

Carefully and quietly listen to My Voice and follow in My Light. If you can and will only recognize My Divine Guidance and know that My Presence is not just a dream, an ideal, a hope, a belief, an aspiration, or even simply an imagination, but that it is *Reality*, then I can lead you into the realization of My Truth. It does not become a Reality to you, however, until you realize it and fully accept it as such in your consciousness. Yet until that time arrives, you can accept in faith in your mind the truth of My Being that you sense in your heart. Then you enable My Presence to grow in your awareness until you fully achieve your Oneness with Me.

If you can recognize My Presence now, we will both rejoice in this achievement; but if you cannot, I will patiently wait until that time when you can and do, just as I have done for centuries past. But only then can I fully bestow upon you the blessings I have to give you, because you must first be able to recognize them and then be open to receive them before I can glorify you with all the overflowing abundance of My Infinite Supply, both spiritual and material.

Because of your past and present desires, you have drawn to yourself what you are reading herein. To this extent you have sought. You are on the threshold. The door into My Light is partly open. You have scarcely a glimpse—no, not more—compared to the unbounded worlds of My Reality that wait within for you. To enter, you have to open wide the door and be able to keep it so. It is necessary that you continue to seek if you want to find an increasing awareness of My Light. And it is true that I freely give to all who sincerely ask. Yet it is a requirement of My Law that you *earn* what you receive; and you earn it by positively responding to My Light in it, by lifting yourself up to it in spiritual consciousness, all of which is the essence of what is meant by asking, seeking, and knocking.

That affinity with Me is achieved by means of your concepts, your desires, your faith, your hope, your consecration, your dedication, your self-discipline, your perseverance—all of the endeavors of your life that enable you to rise to an ever-greater rate of the vibration of My Love. Like tuning your radio to a higher channel, the moment you enter a finer frequency of My Light in consciousness, I freely give to you the full measure of its supply: knowledge, understanding, wisdom, capability, strength, power—whatever it may be, spiritual or material.

Therefore, it is the quality of your present desires, needs, and will as well as your present spiritual consciousness that determines whether or not you are ready to enter your Path of My Light. I Am asking you to follow Me. I Am inviting you onto your Path. I Am encouraging you to seek My Light and

My Love. Yet the decision is your own. I let you be entirely free to come to Me of your own free will. Furthermore, once you enter the Path of My Love, *you* will also determine *how* you will travel it. Will you always listen to My Inner Guidance and consistently, actively follow its bidding, or will you sometimes be careless or wayward as you meet life's temptations along the Way? You know I Am *always* with *you*, but will you always be with Me? Will you always be loyal to Me and to My Light?

Here again, the strength of your desire for the higher Life of My Light and the power of your will to attain it will definitely affect how well you will proceed on your Path of My Love. Using these factors in your life, you will decide whether or not you will permit the negative force of your own soul and of the material world to entice you away into unnecessary detours that will cause you their own degree of heartaches and delays. Only you can make the choice between sealing your fate and fulfilling your Destiny. However, there is one thing here that is certain: How well you learn My Spiritual Laws and how much you obey them will decisively determine your spiritual advancement.

Consequently, as you now know, if you expect to reach your Destiny of Spiritual Mastery safely and successfully, you must learn to recognize reliably, interpret correctly, and follow consistently the guidance of My Still, Small Voice. I have told you that I Am the Way and that I Am the *only* Way to the Kingdom of Heaven—the state of consciousness of the perfect, positive, balanced Polarity of My Spirit. Persistently knock at the entrance of that Way that leads into the higher Life of My Kingdom, deeply desiring to enter. When you lift your material consciousness into My Spiritual Consciousness, you will walk through the Open Door into your Ascension in My Light.

Remember, My Voice within you is not a voice of the material plane; it is a Spiritual Voice, the Voice of your Superconscious Phase of Mind and Spiritual Phase of Body, the Voice of your own God Self, the Voice of the Spiritual Counterpart of your Being. It is the Voice of God, speaking to you through Me. When you live completely in harmony with My Light, your physical voice becomes God's Voice, speaking through Me as I, in turn, speak through you. Both of Us are instruments for His Use. This is another way of showing you that we are One in God when you abide entirely in My Love.

Set the course of your ship of Life and sail east into your rising Sun—the Light of your own Christ Self, the only-begotten Son of God deep within your own Being. Comply with His Counsel at all times, and your ship will carry you into the realm of Spiritual Perfection. No matter what storms may come upon you in your voyage or what trials and tribulations they may bring into your life, steadfastly and valiantly sail on . . . into the Light of your Sun that is ever before you. Even through the darkest clouds, you will see its Light; and as you navigate your ship across your sea of Life, its Light will become ever brighter in your soul until you finally come face to face with the full realization that you are that Sun—that only-begotten Son of God. Then, you will rest in the eternal knowing that I Am you and you are Me.

What you have learned in these pages is only an introductory part of what you need to know to reach your Port of Destiny—Spiritual Mastery. As you listen to My Inner Guidance, pay close attention to all things that My Light brings before you in your soul as well as in your outer material world. I will use all channels open to Me to direct your life in the positive action of My Light. Keep your mind alert to them, and I will lead you, at the proper time, to a school of My Light where I can teach you through others who know My Truth. There you can learn My Spiritual Laws and receive other training you need in order to balance the Positive and Negative Polarity of My Light in your life until you are able to walk alone with Me. It is very important for you to get the spiritual training first, to give you a strong, firm foundation with which to travel your

Path of My Light. In so doing, you will avoid many pitfalls that you may not otherwise be able to escape. Then, as you proceed on your Path of My Light with Me, you will, in time, come to know My Peace.

When you finish this book, lay it down for a while and meditate further upon its substance. Then take it up again and again, studying each chapter thoughtfully until you understand completely its meaning and know well its contents. Each time you do, listen to Me from within you for its deeper interpretation that I will reveal to you. In this way, I can lead you into an ever-greater realization of the message it bears at the same time that I can help you to develop a keener sensitivity to Me, to My Light, and to My Still, Small Voice. And as you practice your Silence and Meditation, taking the stillness of your Silence with you at all times, wherever you go and whatever you do, this awareness of My Presence and My Voice will continually grow deeper in your consciousness, so that I can always afterward safely guide you into your everlasting Destiny of Spiritual Mastery, your Ascension unto Me in My Light. Go on, now, as you walk your Path of My Light in your life, and forever hearken to My Still, Small Voice within the very depth of your own soul. . . . . Be still and listen. . . . . . . Listen. . . . . . . Listen. . . . . . . Then always carefully and steadfastly follow Me. . . . . . .

Interpretation of the Symbolic Diagram of Rishis Institute of Metaphysics *

In the center of the diagram is the smallest, Inner Circle, which is symbolic of God whose center is everywhere and whose circumference is nowhere. The two Pillars portray the Positive and the Negative Polarities, which, when balanced, are God's Light and Energy in perfect equilibrium. This Light, which is God's Creative Power in perfect, infinite expression, is the eternal, positive, harmonious action of Divine Love, the perfection of all Being. The other, larger circles, surrounding the Inner One, depict the various states of consciousness through which all souls progress on their Spiritual Journey toward Union in Consciousness with God through their own indwelling Christ Selves.

The first or lowest state of consciousness is that of the Aspirant or Neophyte. It is signified by the pyramid-like figures whose bases form the outer circle.

*See page i.

It represents the consciousness of the *self* and the narrow, limited view of materiality. In this state of consciousness is the desire to satisfy mainly the personal needs and wants with their lustful inclinations for the carnal, material world, yet now beginning to seek the Higher Spiritual Life of Divine Wisdom and Truth.

The second level is characterized by the largest circular band that symbolizes the budding Disciple growing into a Higher Spiritual Awareness. The small circles within this band typify his consciousness of limitations emerging into an awareness of the Universal Spiritual Laws and Truths.

The third stage is pictured in the second largest round band with wavy lines within it, standing for the Path of the Initiate, the next higher step in Spiritual Unfoldment. The wavy lines illustrate the heights and depths that the human soul experiences as it travels its Path of Self-Discipline and Self-Mastery into its Initiations and consequent Illumination whereby it enters into the higher frequencies of Light that gradually lift it into its Destiny of Spiritual Mastery, the highest attainment mankind can achieve on earth.

The smaller, third, ring-like band, in which the Pillars stand, exemplifies the state of consciousness of the Adept. To become such, it is necessary to balance the two Poles of Positive and Negative Electromagnetic Energy into perfect, positive physical, mental, and emotional expression. This equilibrium must be achieved in order to gain total Mastery of the *self* and the material plane. It is accomplished by lifting and unfolding the lower phases of body and mind into ONENESS IN CONSCIOUSNESS with the Spiritual Phase, the Christ within. This attainment constitutes Spiritual Mastery and the Ascension, portrayed by the fourth or Inner Circle between the pillars, which also represents God.

The Ascension is the process of uniting in consciousness with one's own Superconscious Mind and Spiritual Body, the God Self within, and becoming One in Consciousness with Universal Divine Mind, which is present everywhere in every point of space throughout Infinity and Eternity. It is the ultimate goal of all human souls. Thus, EVERY SOUL, through its evolution of human consciousness, returns to its Source from which it came, though on a Higher Plane, into its heritage of Spiritual Consciousness as a perfected Spiritual Being.

Publications of Rishis
Institute of Metaphysics

BOOKS

THE PATH OF LIGHT by Regina Eveley Lorr and Robert Wall Crary. Publisher: DeVorss & Company. It is an excellent text in Metaphysics that enables anyone to become familiar with the fundamental principles and concepts essential for a clear comprehension of the Spiritual Laws of Life, which are indispensable to any seeker of Truth who desires to follow safely the Path of Light that leads to Spiritual Mastery and the Ascension. It is presented in the form of seven Departments of Life---Spiritual, Mental, Health, Vocational, Financial, Personality, and Domestic---that must be understood and mastered by the aspirant in order to attain this lofty goal, the Destiny of all humankind. (192 pages)

THE STILL SMALL VOICE by Robert Wall Crary. Publisher: Rishis Institute of Metaphysics. Written in the first person, this book introduces the student to the "Voice" of his own Spirit of God within himself and teaches him how to follow it. Also, after providing valuable background information, it presents a detailed description of the Silence and Meditation, taking the student through the Silence, step by step. Then it presents further Metaphysical concepts and understandings, such as Spiritual Mastery, Divine Love, Polarity, Truth, the three phases of Body and Mind, faith, happiness, etc. (210 pages)

MIRACLES IN THE KITCHEN, subtitled Delicious and Nutritious Replacements for Junk Foods, by Regina Eveley Lorr, D.C., D.M., N.D. Publisher: Rishis Institute of Metaphysics. This work is a presentation of a wholistic philosophy of health, dedicated to the purpose of building health, not fighting disease. Thus, physical health is achieved by the use of the natural, raw-food diet, and Dr. Lorr provides an abundance of delicious raw-food recipes to enable all to enjoy fully the food they eat as they follow her Health Program and, at the same time, reap vibrant health. (304 pages)

THE WAY TO SPIRITUAL MASTERY by Robert Wall Crary. Publisher: Rishis Institute of Metaphysics. Herein is depicted the Way everyone must travel his Path of Light. It describes how this Way is universal in the esoteric interpretation of all major religions and of what the scientific mind knows about the universe, though it does so in considerably greater detail for the Christian faith. Beyond this, it

sets forth further metaphysical concepts and understandings, leading the reader into an ever deeper
awareness of Spirit and his own Christ Self within him
at the same time that it alerts and warns him of the
many paths of phenomena that can lead him into
perilous pitfalls and detours and shows him how to
avoid them. (208 pages)

TAPE

THE VOICE OF THE SILENCE by Robert Wall
Crary and Regina Eveley Lorr. Publisher: Rishis Institute of Metaphysics. This tape introduces the student to the "Voice" of the Spirit of God, the Silence,
and Meditation. As it is played, after giving background information about all three, it leads the listener
into and through the Silence, step by step, enabling
him to enter and dwell in the Silence and Meditation as
he listens. The voice of the tape is accompanied by
pleasant, quieting, relaxing background music along
with positive subliminal affirmations relating to relaxation and positive response to Light. (Approximately 90
minutes)